FUGITIVE MAN

FUGITIVE MAN

HUNTING VIOLENT CRIMINALS FOR THE FBI
and
SEARCHING FOR JUSTICE FOR THE INNOCENT CONVICT

Robert K. Cromwell

FBI SPECIAL AGENT IN CHARGE (RETIRED)
CHAIRMAN, INNOCENCE PROJECT OF FLORIDA

MCP Books, Minneapolis, MN

Copyright © 2016 by Robert K. Cromwell

MCP Books
322 First Avenue N, 5th Floor
Minneapolis, MN 55401
612.455.2293
www.mcpbooks.com

All rights reserved. No part of this publication may be reproduced, stored in a retrieval system, or transmitted, in any form or by any means, electronic, mechanical, photocopying, recording, or otherwise, without the prior written permission of the author.

Note: The opinions expressed herein are those of the author and not those of the Federal Bureau of Investigation. The Federal Bureau of Investigation does not endorse, approve, or authorize this publication.

ISBN-13: 978-1-63505-079-0
LCCN: 2016907881

Distributed by Itasca Books

Cover Design by C. Tramell
Typeset by Robert Harmon

Printed in the United States of America

To my brother, Retired Princeton Township Police Captain David Cromwell, who set the example that started me on my way to a great law enforcement career.

And to my dear wife, Rosa Lee Cromwell, who for more than 40 years has always had more confidence in me than I've had in myself. Thank you, Rosa.

"Certainly there is no hunting like the hunting of man and those who have hunted armed men long enough and liked it, never really care for anything else thereafter."

(Ernest Hemingway, "On the Blue Water," 1936)

Jeffrey Holt – UFAP – Kidnapping, Robbery, Rape, Attempted Murder

Jeffrey Holt was wanted for Unlawful Flight to Avoid Prosecution (UFAP) for kidnapping, robbery, rape and attempted murder. Late one evening Holt had broken into a young woman's home in central California and had brutally raped, tortured, kidnaped and attempted to murder her. He had almost been successful.

When I first heard of him, Holt had been on the run for some time. Using information provided by the Sacramento Division of the FBI, and working with other reliable sources, I developed a lead on Holt at his potential place of employment. Holt worked under an assumed name in the restaurant of a hotel several miles south of Houston. He was one of the hotel's friendly bartenders. Another agent and I went to the bar, played some pool, drank some iced tea, and waited for Jeffrey's arrival. Jeff strolled in just in time to start his shift. We grabbed him before he could don his apron. When confronted, he admitted his identity and was handcuffed, searched, and taken into custody without incident.

After his arrest, we transported Holt back to the Houston FBI office. After taking off his handcuffs, we sat down with Jeffrey, and I read him his Constitutional Rights. He stated he understood his rights, he did not want to speak with an attorney, signed the Advice of Rights form, and declared he was willing to talk. We then started talking. We talked about the Houston Rockets and the Houston Astros, we talked bartending (something I knew nothing about), and we talked of my experiences in the Navy. We did not speak of the crimes he was accused of for some time. After several minutes, I sent a new agent, who was sitting in on the interview with me, off to get a can of Pepsi for Jeffrey. The new agent came back with the Pepsi and asked if he could see me in the hall. I walked out, and he said, "Bob, why are you being nice to that shitbird? I can't stand being in the same room with him." I told him to just bear with me; we would talk about it later. I then returned, and Jeffrey and I continued our friendly conversation.

After several minutes of talk to get the point across to Jeffrey that I thought he was a decent person, I finally got around to the crime. Since we had treated him well and developed a good rapport, he seemed convinced that we thought he was a regular guy who had simply made a serious mistake. I made it clear that we wanted to offer him some help, but I also suggested that he needed to offer an explanation for his outrageous behavior. It wasn't as if I was asking him if he did it. I was just trying to let him see that we knew he was not a bad person, that we knew he had committed the crimes for which he'd been arrested, but that we also knew that it must have been an out-of-character mistake, one which he simply needed to explain.

After much hesitation, he confessed that he had a drug problem and explained that, on the night of the crime, he had been high. He admitted that he had observed the attractive victim through her window and had climbed through that window into her home. He then asserted the rest of the night was a blank. He claimed that he couldn't remember what he had actually done to her. However, that was all we (and the prosecutor) needed.

After lodging Jeffrey in the Harris County Jail in downtown Houston, I spoke with the new agent about his impatience and dislike of sitting with Holt. I explained that we might have just prevented the victim in this case from having to go to trial. Furthermore, if Holt hadn't confessed, his defense attorney would have tried to make the victim look somehow responsible for the events of that horrible evening, and going to trial could have been akin to another atrocious assault on the woman.

As of this writing, Jeffrey Holt remains an inmate in the California Department of Corrections.

IX

U.S. Department of Justice

Federal Bureau of Investigation

In Reply, Please Refer to
File No.

Post Office Box 13130
Sacramento, California 95813

December 19, 1988

Mr. Andrew J. Duffin
Special Agent in Charge
Federal Bureau of Investigation
Houston, Texas

Dear Andy,

    I would like to express my appreciation for the work of Special Agent Robert W. Cromwell of your division regarding the capture of the fugitive Jeffrey Darin Holt on December 16, 1988 in Houston, Texas.

    Subject Holt was wanted by the FBI for unlawful flight to avoid prosecution. Holt had fled California after raping, kidnapping, torturing, and attempting to murder a Department of Justice employee. This particular employee had worked with the Sacramento Division of the FBI on numerous cases and was highly regarded.

    Throughout the investigation SA Cromwell instituted surveillances, obtained telephone records, and interviewed the subscribers which eventually lead to the arrest of subject Holt. The confession obtained by SA Cromwell may allow prosecution of subject Holt without the case going to court and the victim ever having to face the emotional trauma of testifying.

    My congratulations to Agent Cromwell on a job well done.

Sincerely,

TERRY L. KNOWLES
Special Agent in Charge

DEC 27 1988
FBI — HOUSTON

INTRODUCTION

After six years as a Cryptology Technician in the Navy, I spent a year at the College of New Jersey finishing my bachelor's degree before becoming a New Jersey police officer. A few years later, I became an NCIS special agent and, finally, an FBI special agent. I spent 22 years in the FBI. For more than half of those years, I worked within the FBI's Violent Crime Program. For eight of those years, I principally hunted violent fugitives in Houston, Texas. That's a great place to hunt fugitives, and I was good at it. It was addictive. Throughout my career, nothing really came close to the kick I got out of tracking down and catching a fugitive. I still miss it, but realistically know I would be hard pressed to run and climb over the fences I once climbed in Houston.

I also had a talent for getting people to talk and a knack for developing informants. The two go hand in hand. Outstanding informants were one of the reasons I was able to make so many arrests. In developing good informants to find fugitives, I found it especially important to learn to move amongst Houston's street people and the people serving, selling, and sometimes exploiting them. Many of the violent people we were attempting to take off the street were preying on unfortunate street people, many of who suffered from significant mental disabilities. It remains true to this day. Numerous homeless people suffer from post-traumatic stress disorder, schizophrenia, bipolar disease, and often substance abuse. Frequently, the fugitives we hunted, while hiding from the law, were taking advantage of those most vulnerable people. Through regular and repeated contacts, I got to know some of the dedicated men and women providing services to those street people and eventually convinced many that our taking violent fugitives off the street represented a clear benefit to their clientele. Ultimately, trust blossomed, and many of those serving the homeless, and even some of the homeless themselves, helped us discover fugitives' whereabouts. It was good for everyone involved, except, of course, the fugitives.

I enjoyed many successes over the course of several years, developed great sources and made many arrests. In 1991 I received a commendation and cash award from

U.S. Department of Justice

Federal Bureau of Investigation

Office of the Director

Washington, D.C. 20535

May 23, 1991

PERSONAL

Mr. Robert K. Cromwell
Federal Bureau of Investigation
Houston, Texas

Dear Mr. Cromwell:

    It is certainly a pleasure to acknowledge your achievements in the Fugitive Program in the Houston Division, and you are to be commended. In addition, I would like to present you with the enclosed cash award as a token of my appreciation.

    Your dedication, tenacity, and talent can be attributed to the success achieved in the Fugitive Program. Your resoucefulness and diligent efforts have led to the development of symbol sources, the establishment of contacts within the law enforcement and secular communities, and leading the division in arrests for the past five years. Displaying exceptional professional ability, foresight, and mature judgment, you have guided this program as the most proficient in the Nation, and the selflessness with which you gave of your time and effort in this matter are most praiseworthy. You should be proud of your achievements.

Sincerely yours,

William S. Sessions
Director

Enclosure

Director of the FBI, for making the Houston fugitive program the "most proficient in the Nation" and for leading the Houston Division in arrests for five consecutive years.

The fact that I led the division in arrests for five years sounds good and was certainly a commendable accomplishment, but it should be put in context. Many outstanding agents investigate complex cases for months, or even years, before making an arrest. Most of my cases involved tracking people down, taking them into custody, trying to get them to talk, and then turning them over to the U.S. Marshal's Service or local sheriff's department for transfer to the jurisdiction where their crime was committed. Additionally, many excellent FBI agents work in the intelligence or counterterrorism arena for years, even decades, doing exceptional and very important work without ever making an arrest. So, while I was proud of my award from the director and loved what I was doing, I knew I was one of many agents doing good work for the FBI.

By most any measure, I had significant law enforcement experience on which to call, starting as a street cop and ending as the Special Agent in Charge of one of the FBI's 56 field divisions. I've arrested many criminals, and I recognize that the overwhelming majority of people convicted and sent to prison are guilty. However, I've also come to learn that many innocent people are in prison as well. After retiring from the FBI at the end of 2005, I became acquainted with the Innocence Project of Florida and recognized the great work they were doing in attempting to exonerate innocent people through DNA testing and other means. These are not people who are just "technically innocent"; they are actual innocent people who have been convicted and imprisoned for crimes they did not commit. Since 2007, I have been on the Board of Directors of the Innocence Project of Florida. (www.floridainnocence.org). I give my time and money to help the Innocence Project because the Innocence Project's mission is clearly in the best interest of justice. I simply find it unconscionable for us to ignore the innocent who are in prison for crimes they did not commit.

Our criminal justice system desperately needs some fine-tuning. Near the end of this book, I have provided a few simple recommendations on modifying critical investigative practices. The International Association of Chiefs of Police, an organization of which I am a Life Member, supports many similar recommendations. It's time every law enforcement agency adopts those changes. It's a matter of fundamental fairness and, in many cases, the difference between incarceration and freedom for an innocent person. (And every innocent person in jail may equate to a guilty violent person on the street, preying on the public.)

CHAPTER ONE

BACKGROUND

After fulfilling my Navy enlistment and obtaining my Bachelor's Degree, I had the good fortune to spend nearly four years as a Montgomery Township police officer. Montgomery Township is a central New Jersey community bordering Princeton, Rocky Hill, Hillsborough Township, Hopewell Township, and Franklin Township.

The patrol officer has one of the most dangerous jobs in law enforcement. I arrested hundreds of violent felons during my time with the FBI, many more than most police officers do in a career, but I had a huge advantage. I always knew I was confronting a felon, a person considered "armed and dangerous." I approached each arrest as a tactical problem and, with few exceptions, had another agent with me. Additionally, I attempted to arrange things so the first time a fugitive was concerned about my presence, I had the drop on him, and he was staring at my badge and weapon pointed at him from a short distance away. That, typically, made for cooperative fugitives and a safer working environment.

In contrast, many police officers on patrol routinely pull over traffic offenders, respond to alarms, and handle domestic disturbance calls alone. The officer stopping a traffic violator never knows if he or she is pulling over a mom late to pick up her kids from school or a felon who just shot someone or robbed a bank. The majority of traffic stops are non-events, which often leads to a false sense of security or comfort zone that can be shattered in an instant. Traffic stops really are one of the most dangerous jobs in law enforcement.

While police officers on patrol are in a hazardous line of work, the police officer's job also has its lighter moments. One evening, I found myself behind a vehicle traveling slowly and swerving all over the road. I activated the overhead lights on my patrol car, and the vehicle in front of me pulled onto the edge of a lawn. I approached and found myself face to face with a 70-something-year-old lady, nicely dressed as if coming from church. She smelled of alcohol and was obviously impaired. I helped her out of the car and quickly determined she was having a hard time standing. She informed me that she had consumed a "bit of wine" with her lady friends. I took her back to police headquarters, sat her down in an interview room, and started to warm up the breathalyzer, the machine used for checking a person's blood alcohol level. In those days, the machine had to warm up for twenty minutes before a test could be conducted, so as the machine warmed up, I filled out paperwork.

As I prepared the documents inherent to her arrest, the little old lady just sat across from me, swaying back and forth, patiently waiting to blow into the Breathalyzer. However, after a few minutes, her rocking motion ceased, and she leaned forward, across the table, and stared at my chest. I wasn't exactly sure what she was looking at until she said, "Cromwell…are you related to the undertaker in Hopewell?" She had noticed my nametag. I said, "Yes, John Cromwell is my father's cousin."

The sweet old lady then began, "Oh, he is such a nice man. A few years ago, he buried my husband, and he couldn't have been nicer to me." She got a bit more animated and a bit louder, stating, "But I've known John Cromwell since he was a little boy, and you can ask anyone in Hopewell, and they'll tell you what a nice man John Cromwell is!"

I thought for a moment what a sweet little old drunk lady she was. Then, after hesitating just a moment, she added, "You know, I just can't believe he's related to a son-of-a-bitch like you!" I laughed out loud and so did she.

Looking back, nice old ladies or not, drunk drivers are a serious threat to the rest of us and must be taken off the street, so I have no regrets regarding the many DUIs I locked up while an officer. However, if I had it to do over again, I would have been a little easier on young people committing minor driving infractions. Having now raised three sons with my wife, and knowing many sad stories behind the lives of many kids with whom I've come in contact, I would have been more understanding with the teenagers I dealt with while a police officer. Many of them had it tough at home and could have used more understanding and compassion than I sometimes provided as the "son-of-a-bitch" cop I was.

One particularly valuable lesson learned during my time in Montgomery occurred while participating in a sexual assault investigation. It is a lesson that has stuck with me to this day. The victim, a woman in her late teens, gave a detailed description of the assailant's vehicle including that it had an orange exterior and black interior. The vehicle also had unusual door locking mechanisms, which she described as "light switches turned sideways." She also recalled that the vehicle had three rotting apple cores on the front passenger floorboard.

Our investigation determined that the vehicle was very likely a Dodge Colt, and an inquiry with the New Jersey Division of Motor Vehicles revealed only 35 orange/black Colts registered in the State of New Jersey. The victim also sat down with a police artist and provided a description of the assailant, resulting in a drawing of the suspect being circulated throughout the area.

We quickly identified as a suspect a young man who lived in a nearby community and owned an orange/black Dodge Colt. His vehicle was the correct model and color. He also looked like he could have posed for the artist's drawing. His alibi for the time of the assault was weak. The icing on the cake occurred when I walked by his car late at night and clearly saw three rotting apple cores on the passenger side floorboard. The assistant county attorney, the other investigators, and I all felt we had our man.

We were wrong.

As we were driving our suspect to the county attorney's office to participate in a court-ordered lineup, we received a radio call notifying us that another guy who looked like the drawing of the suspect and who was also driving the somewhat unique orange and black Dodge Colt had been stopped by one of our patrol cars. (By the way, statistically, officers on patrol are the ones who solve most crimes.) Rotting apple cores were observed on the vehicle's floorboard. In a subsequent lineup featuring both suspects, the victim immediately identified the guy picked up by the patrol officer as her assailant. While the police artist's drawing favored the innocent subject, our victim was unequivocal when seeing both the actual subject and our incorrect subject in a lineup.

The actual perpetrator admitted to having had sex with our victim but claimed the sex was consensual, so we knew we had the right guy. However, after a contentious trial, the subject was acquitted.

I learned quite a lesson. We certainly had enough evidence to indict our innocent suspect, and had our victim been accidently killed before picking the true perpetrator out of a lineup, we might have done so. The sketch of the assailant looked more like our suspect than the actual perpetrator. A jury might have convicted him. But he was innocent. It's something I've kept in mind ever since.

I had the pleasure of working with some great people on the police force. One of them, Chuck Person, was particularly sharp and had a great, dry sense of humor. One evening, as I was coming on the midnight shift and Chuck was getting off, we spent a few minutes on patrol together, discussing the goings-on in the community. After checking the front of a shopping center, we drove down the alley behind the center, checking the back doors on the left. As we did so, a man came out of the bushes ahead of us on the right. He was hopping, with his hands and ankles bound, and was gagged. As we drove along the alley after observing the guy in front of us, Chuck raised an eyebrow and, sounding a bit like Dirty Harry, quietly stated, "We should probably check him out." We did. The guy was a restaurant manager who had been robbed at gunpoint while making the night deposit. In that obviously serious and perhaps dangerous situation, Chuck made me laugh.

CHAPTER TWO

N.C.I.S.
THE NAVAL CRIMINAL INVESTIGATIVE SERVICE

During six years as a Cryptology Technician in the Navy, with most of my time working for NSA, I never crossed paths with the Naval Investigative Service. However, as a police officer, I had a couple of encounters with them and was impressed by the agents I met and the scope of investigations NIS agents addressed. In 1981, I resigned from the police department to become a special agent with NIS. The name was subsequently changed to the Naval Criminal Investigative Service, or NCIS, as seen on the CBS hit dramas. Being an NCIS agent was much like being an FBI agent for the Navy and Marine Corps. The investigations and paperwork inherent to them were similar to the FBI. It turned out to be a great organization to be part of if you eventually wanted to be an FBI Agent, but that was certainly not my intention when joining up.

Assigned to a two-agent Resident Unit at the Portsmouth Naval Shipyard in Kittery, Maine, I was teamed with John Hajosy, a senior, seasoned NIS agent and one of the sharpest investigators with whom I ever worked. He was patient and took his time to show me how things were done. He also had a killer sense of humor, routinely answered Mensa trivia questions, and was fond of bird watching. He impressed me as a modern day Renaissance man. The good fortune of being assigned to Portsmouth with John Hajosy proved to be one of the best learning experiences of my career.

My work at NIS included, among other things, investigating violent crime, foreign counterintelligence, fraud against the government, and drug offences. Using cooperating witnesses and undercover officers, we were involved in many illegal drug investigations, as we at NIS Portsmouth viewed anyone selling drugs in the Portsmouth, New Hampshire/Kittery, Maine, area as a potential threat to the many military personnel present in the area.

Around the time I joined NCIS in 1981, the Navy introduced random urinalysis as a deterrent to illegal drug use. Through source information, we learned three young Marines had found a way to circumvent the urinalysis program.

They imported, sold, and used LSD.

At that time, the Navy's urinalysis protocol was not sensitive to LSD. As a result, the Portsmouth Naval Shipyard had the potential for Marines armed with .45 caliber pistols to be guarding nuclear submarines while tripping on LSD. We determined that the LSD was being imported from Detroit by three junior Marines for a dollar a tablet and was thereafter sold for $4.00 a tablet to civilians, while military personnel received a *"military discount"* and could purchase the tablets for $3.00 apiece. The investigation was intense, employing three young Marines in undercover capacities making several purchases of LSD from each of the three sellers. I admired those three Marines as brave young men doing the right thing in the best interest of the Marine Corps.

Late one night, I met one of the Marines working with us at a Rest Area on I-95, a few miles north of the Maine/New Hampshire border, to recover LSD he purchased that evening. The young Marine arrived on his motorcycle, and I quickly realized he was high as a kite. He behaved in a manic-depressive manner, one minute laughing and the next crying. I had developed a good working relationship with the young Marine. Like most Marines he really had his act together, and I was quite sure he had not intentionally taken anything. I found myself in a quandary. Taking him to a military hospital might jeopardize the investigation, but I didn't feel comfortable not seeking medical advice. I therefore took him to a civilian hospital where I spoke with a doctor about the situation, received some reassurance, and obtained a urine sample from the Marine. I then spent several hours with him until he came down from his LSD-induced high. The next morning, I spoke with the Armed Forces Institute of Pathology (AFIP) in Washington and discovered they could examine the urine to determine if the Marine had in fact consumed LSD. A week later, AFIP confirmed the presence of LSD in the Marine's urine.

At the completion of the investigation, 18 Marines faced general courts-martial, 15 for using LSD and three for using and selling it. All were convicted. The fifteen users were demoted, received bad conduct discharges, fines, and minor jail sentences. The three dealers were sentenced to seven years hard labor, demoted to E1, made to forfeit all pay and benefits, and given Dishonorable Discharges. One of the three also was also convicted of aggravated assault for having crushed LSD into the food of his fellow Marine, our informant. While going to jail and being dishonorably discharged was a heavy hit for that young man, it seemed to him that the most severe punishment was losing his classic '67 Ford Mustang. Since he used the vehicle in the furtherance of his drug business, we used Maine state law to seize it. John Hajosy and I turned the pristine vehicle over to the Maine State Police at high noon, at the front gate of the shipyard, so all the Marines present for the changing of the guard could see the Mustang being driven away by a Maine state police officer.

While no Marine desires to be an "informer" on his fellow Marines, the outlandish nature of the three Marines selling LSD to 15 armed Marines and the 15 armed Marines using LSD was an affront to all the Marines on base, and many of the young Marines let us know they appreciated our efforts. As one example, soon after the courts-martial conclusions, I was walking up the front steps of the Marine barracks to visit their CO. A group of about 12 off-duty Marines were relaxing on the balcony area of the second deck. When they saw me, the 12 stood at attention and applauded. They clearly agreed with our cleaning up their barracks. I have a tremendous respect for the Marines. As an enlisted man in the Navy, and while an NCIS agent, I observed the Marines to be a most impressive group of brave young men and women, displaying great discipline. And most of the young Marines I knew had their act together and rarely got in any serious trouble.

UNITED STATES MARINE CORPS
MARINE BARRACKS, UNITED STATES NAVAL SHIPYARD
PORTSMOUTH, NEW HAMPSHIRE. 03801

IN REPLY REFER TO
DTW:jav -
5000
7 June 1983

Director
Naval Investigative Service
Washington, D. C. 20388

Dear Sir,

This letter is to express my appreciation to the Naval Investigative Service for outstanding job accomplishment regarding a drug investigation here at Marine Barracks, Portsmouth Naval Shipyard. Early in March of this year, when information regarding drugs surfaced, Marine sources were referred to the local NIS office. Upon request, agents John Hajosy and Bob Cromwell immediately opened the investigations and with Mr. Cromwell as the primary investigator, work began with the Marine sources.

By the end of May, an exhaustive and thorough investigation was completed and forwarded to this Command. As a result, disciplinary action is underway and the drug problem which existed at this Barracks has been eliminated.

Throughout the entire period of this investigation, the cooperation received from the local NIS office was exceptional. In particular I would like to commend Mr. Cromwell for the many, many hours put into this case and for his professional handling of all aspects of the investigation.

On numerous occasions, both Mr. Cromwell and Mr. Hajosy were called out late at night to meet with the sources. Their efforts on behalf of this Command are sincerely appreciated. With cooperation like this we will demonstrate that drugs are not tolerated in the military services.

Respectfully,

D. T. WELSH
Lieutenant Colonel, U. S. Marine Corps
Commanding

NCIS occasionally provided protection for foreign diplomats and other dignitaries at the request of the Department of Defense, State Department, Secret Service, and other agencies. After being an NCIS agent for a year or two, I was sent to Dignitary Protection School in Virginia. It sounded like fun and turned out to be an eye-opening experience and one that gave me a newfound appreciation for the U.S. Secret Service.

As part of my training, I became qualified to use an Uzi submachine gun. As one of the Uzi men for a motorcade, I was responsible for exiting my vehicle and "clearing" the area on my side of the road. After determining there were no threats present, my nod alerted the team leader that my side was clear.

We practiced different ingress and egress scenarios with an instructor role-playing as the dignitary. On one occasion we pulled up to a home in the country with the goal of safely delivering our dignitary to the inside of the residence. I exited the vehicle on the passenger's side, across the street from the country home, and carefully surveyed the brush and mostly-wooded area on my side of the vehicle. After noting nothing of a threatening nature, I gave my nod to indicate my side was clear.

Boy, was I wrong! The scenario was halted, and the instructor approached me and verified that I thought the area on my side of the road was clear. I so verified. To my utter amazement, from the low shrubs not more than ten yards away, appeared a Marine sniper in full ghillie suit. (A ghillie suit, also known as a yowie suit, or camo tent, is camouflage clothing designed to resemble heavy foliage.) He blended with the terrain so well that I had no hint of him until he moved. Had it been a real protection detail, the dignitary and the rest of us would have been toast. The sniper's ability to blend into the ground amazed me.

During that training, I visited the FBI Academy in Quantico for the first time. I was taken there to become qualified with the Uzi. After becoming Uzi qualified, I learned that, should an ambush of a motorcade occur, the Uzi man's job was to get out and draw fire as the motorcade sped away. My first thought was that they could keep their Uzi. Call me crazy, but being left behind to draw fire did not appeal to me in the slightest.

However, I know from experience that people react in a stressful situation the way they're trained. That's one of the reasons the agents of the Secret Service are so good in their protection role. To go towards a shooter or to jump in front of a weapon to shield someone is not a rational thing to do, but it's what Secret Service men and women are constantly trained for. Therefore, when one of their protectees is threatened, that training takes over, and the Secret Service perform their job with bravery of the highest nature.

The Portsmouth Naval Shipyard repairs submarines. The submarine service attracts some of the brightest people in the Navy. Sometimes, though, even they do something horrific. Late one evening, I responded to a reported stabbing in one of the women's quarters on base. A young Navy woman had been stabbed and slashed. She was critically wounded. She lost a lot of blood. I spoke with her as she was being moved by medics from her quarters and, again, briefly in the ambulance, and I was able to get a statement from her identifying who stabbed her. The young man, whose advances had been spurned by the victim, had come to her quarters to give her "a going away present," since he and his submarine were leaving early the next morning. He told her to close her eyes, and when she did, he stabbed her in the abdomen and proceeded to slash her in several locations. She almost bled out, but ultimately she survived and recovered.

My partner, John Hajosy, was on an infrequent trip out of town, so I grabbed one of the shipyard police detectives and quickly went to the assailant's submarine, looking to make an apprehension. Since the submarine was leaving in the early morning, its nuclear plant was up and running. Because of this, there were Radiation Control or "RADCON" officers on the dock to verify that everyone boarding the ship had a Thermo-Luminescent-Dosimeter, or TLD, to measure radiation exposure. The RADCON officer attempted to stop me at the dock, "Where's your TLD?" Cavalierly, I stuck my NIS badge in the guy's face and said, "Here's my TLD," and strolled onto the sub.

That was a mistake. I broke several rules and regulations by busting on through security to get that sailor. Thank God the slasher was onboard. The Captain of the sub was very grateful that I removed the assailant quickly off his ship, and I ultimately got away with a "good job" and "don't do that again." The sailor, court martialed in New Haven, CT, received eight years hard labor and a bad conduct discharge.

CHAPTER THREE

THE FBI

Graduation from FBI New Agents Training, 1984.

NCIS promised a great career, and it wasn't easy to leave. Especially considering I had two sons and my wife was pregnant with our third. If I had been injured during FBI new agent training or had flunked out, I might have been out of work. It was simply a matter of me wanting to be part of what's been touted as the greatest law enforcement agency in the world. Three decades later, I can tell you it was a good move.

I resigned from NIS and joined the FBI in January 1984. I entered the FBI Academy in Quantico, VA, and found myself in a class of very accomplished people. Quite frankly,

I sometimes wondered what I was doing there, surrounded by such talent, including lawyers, accountants and scientists. However, making it through that storied law enforcement academy was a great confidence builder.

After graduating from the Academy, my wife and I, along with our three sons (our third, Johnny, was born after I had been in Quantico for two weeks), moved to Houston, Texas.

We spent eight years in Houston. My primary focus there was violent crime, with a focus on violent fugitives. At that time, the FBI considered a violent fugitive someone who was wanted for Unlawful Flight to Avoid Prosecution (UFAP) or Unlawful Flight to Avoid Confinement (UFAC) for violent crimes, including murder, attempted murder, kidnaping, rape, robbery, arson, aggravated assault, and burglary of a habitation. Houston is the third or fourth largest city in the United States. It is huge, and it's a place where many people migrate for work and some migrate to hide. I was a young, aggressive FBI agent, and I discovered I had a knack for finding people. It was a rewarding experience, taking bad people off the street. I had the time of my life.

CHAPTER FOUR

ARTHUR REED COLLUM
UFAP - MURDER, ARMED ROBBERY

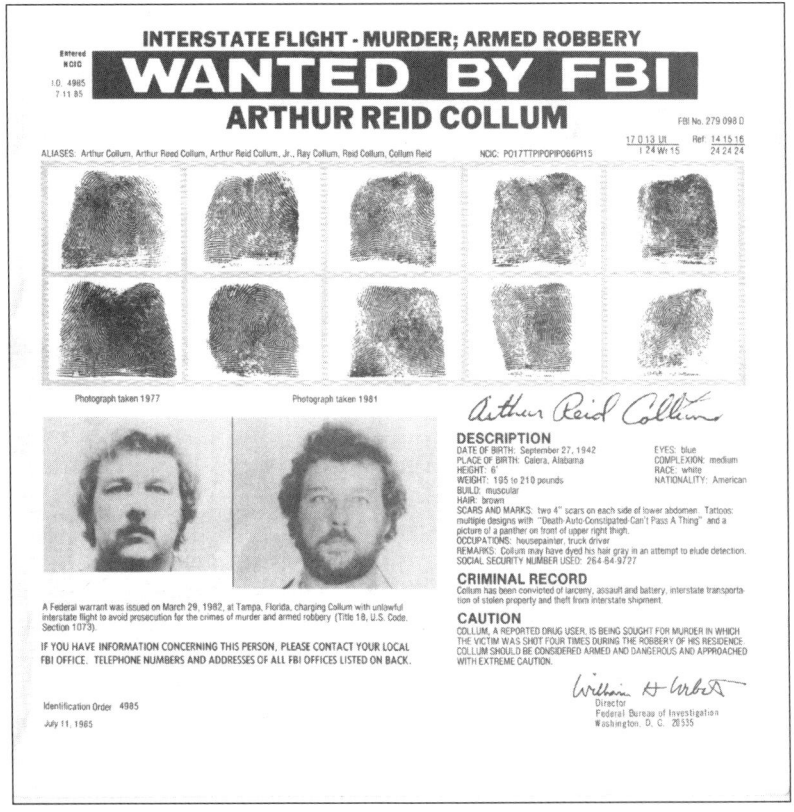

Prior to shooting a man to death and fleeing Florida, Arthur Reid Collum had assisted the FBI with several criminal investigations. I was told by an agent in the Tampa Division that after Collum was indicted in Tampa for armed robbery and murder, and the FBI obtained a UFAP-Murder warrant for him, local Tampa police officials doubted the FBI would try very hard to catch him as they had heard of Colum's prior relationship with the Bureau.

One type of FBI wanted poster, called an "Identification Order (IO)," is only issued for the most sought after fugitives in the nation. When I was in the Bureau, there were usually less than 80 active IOs outstanding in the country at any given time. They're sent to virtually every police and sheriff's department in the US, Canada, and several other nations. They're what you sometimes see on the wall at your local post office. At the request of the Tampa Division, FBIHQ issued an IO on Collum.

Collum was one of my cases. Through my investigation, which included information obtained from informants I developed, I found a payphone used by Collum in a hardware store in the affluent West University area of Houston. After spending time observing the hardware store, I visited the store and determined through observation and interview that Collum was not employed there. However, a store employee was fairly certain he recognized Collum's photo as that of a house painter who purchased supplies in the store. The employee also provided me a description of the Collum's van.

Following exhaustive searching through nearby neighborhoods, we located the parked suspect van, and kept it under surveillance for a couple hours. Eventually, a man resembling Collum and an attractive young woman came out of an apartment, both wearing painter's coveralls. They entered the van and departed. Agent Phil Stukes and I followed the van into an exclusive West University neighborhood, west of downtown Houston. When the van pulled into the driveway of a beautiful home, we followed into the driveway, exited our vehicle with our weapons drawn, and arrested Arthur Reid Collum without incident. ("Without incident" is how arrests are supposed to go. When there's an "incident," there's going to be a ton of paperwork and the possibility of headquarters drilling into the case to see what you did wrong. "Without incident" were two of my favorite words.)

Prior to the arrest, I advised the Tampa case agent that we were getting close to Collum. He advised me that Collum was very "slick" and not likely to say anything about the crime for which he was being arrested. When we took him to the office, Collum was receptive to conversation, and we spoke about his painting business in Houston and a number of other topics. He was a pleasant guy, and establishing rapport was easy. He was quite proud of the interior paintwork he was doing in high-end Houston homes and told us so. We bought him a soda and listened with interest as he discussed with pleasure a couple of his most recent jobs, one of which had appeared in a Houston area home décor magazine.

After a half hour or so of conversation, I produced an Advice of Rights form and asked him if he would like to talk about "the mess in Tampa." He replied, "Bob, I'd like to talk to you about it, but I better talk to my attorney first."

That was the end of the interview. Once Collum invoked his right to an attorney, we could no longer ask him questions about the crime. I continued to fill out paperwork, and he continued to speak about other, non-crime-related matters. After several minutes, Collum looked over at the IO on my desk with his photo on it and said, "You mind if I look at that?" I said, "No, not at all," and handed it to him. He reviewed the IO and announced, "You know, it says here I shot the guy four times. It doesn't mention he tried to stab me first."

That unsolicited "spontaneous utterance" was a confession. I couldn't ask any follow-up questions and didn't say anything to him about what he had just said, but I knew the prosecutor in the case would be pleased by Collum's comment (and I was likely going to visit Tampa for the first time.)

Ultimately, I flew to Tampa to testify at Collum's trial. It was an unusual situation. Two agents who had handled Collum were there as reluctant defense witnesses to testify about the work Collum performed for the FBI. Collum's spontaneous utterance in Houston played well in the trial, and Collum had to admit he shot the victim, but he used the defense that he was working for the FBI when he killed the victim in self-defense. The jury didn't buy that. Collum was convicted of murder in 1988 and sentenced to life in prison without parole. In March 2005, Arthur died while in the custody of the Florida Department of Corrections.

This case is a good example of where the patient development of rapport, even without a chance to ask questions and minimize or rationalize the crime, still led to the subject providing damaging evidence against his interests. It also points out how very important it is to listen.

CHAPTER FIVE

SPINS

My Houston FBI squad also handled Civil Rights investigations and certain background investigations. There were a couple of agents on the squad who addressed the lion's share of the background caseload. However, I sometimes found myself in one of the worst parts of town in the morning, arresting a fugitive, and then in one of the nicest parts of town in the afternoon, conducting a SPIN interview.

SPINs are "Special Inquiries." They are background investigations of individuals being considered for a Presidential appointment to a job requiring Senate confirmation. Those are the highest-level positions in the federal government, such as Cabinet members, federal district, appeal, and Supreme Court judges, Ambassadors, etc. SPINs are in-depth inquiries, and the finished product is voluminous. No stone is left unturned, and influential people on both sides of the aisle are queried as to their relationship and/or experience with the nominee. Many potential high-level appointees have not made the cut due to revelations obtained during SPINs. The investigations are extremely time-sensitive and are closely overseen by FBI Headquarters. George H.W. Bush was Vice President, and then President, during my time in Houston, and Houston was his home. As a result, we had many presidential appointees with Houston connections.

I met many interesting people while conducting SPINs, but the person I remember most is the late John Connolly. As the Governor of Texas in 1963, he sat in the limousine across from President John F. Kennedy and was shot and seriously wounded when President Kennedy was assassinated. The Governor also served as the Secretary of the Navy under President Kennedy and was Secretary of the Treasury under President Richard Nixon. Governor Connolly received visits on many SPINs as he had extensive experience serving our country, was very well informed, and seemed to know everyone. In fact, he appeared to know who the subject of the next SPIN would be before we even received the assignment. Conversing with the Governor was always interesting and informative. He was a very bright and personable gentleman.

Once, while visiting with him and discussing a potential appointee, Governor Connolly delivered a bulletin: "The President's going to nominate (former Senator) John Tower for Secretary of Defense. The shit is going to hit the fan. But he would still be a good Secretary of Defense." The Governor was correct about the potential nomination coming, the shit did hit the fan, and Mr. Tower never had the opportunity to serve as the Secretary of Defense as the Senate voted not to confirm him to the position.

While working violent crime cases, I met some very interesting people, but few were as interesting as Governor Connolly. It was a great experience meeting with him, and he's a person I'll always remember. It's also an example of what a great job being an FBI agent is. You can be chasing killers in the morning and having iced tea with the former Secretary of the Treasury in the afternoon.

CHAPTER SIX

HOUSTON SWAT

After about a year in the Houston Division, I tried out and was chosen for the Houston SWAT team. I attended the FBI SWAT School at Quantico. It was two weeks of good tactical training. Our highly competent SWAT school leader provided us with wax bullets he crafted in his oven at home. I don't believe the commercially made and softer, simulated ammo had yet hit the market. We wore vests, goggles, and throat protectors, but when you were hit by one of those wax bullets it stung like hell, which was about as close to being shot as you could get without drawing blood. (Although, come to think of it, they sometimes did draw blood.) It made for very realistic, heart-pounding training. During the school, we went through a ton of ammo on the range, we repelled down buildings and off helicopter's skids, we navigated through the woods to locate a pre-determined position, and we planned and executed many entries into multiple rooms and other confined spaces.

The SWAT training gave me a more focused view of issues that come with making entries into homes to seek out potentially armed and dangerous individuals. It was therefore good training for me, as I was working violent crime and chasing fugitives. Another practical reason was transportation. When I arrived in Houston, there were insufficient vehicles available to the agents, and vehicles were shared. It proved inconvenient and often a barrier to productivity. As a new agent, the chances of me having my own take-home car were about zero. However, a benefit of being on the SWAT team was having your own vehicle. It made my life easier, and made me more efficient.

In Houston, the SWAT team practiced once or twice a month and focused on developing and maintaining the ability to make quick entries into most types of structures, and using overwhelming firepower to quickly free hostages and render the area safe. The training called for repetition in practicing quick and coordinated entries, being able to discriminate the good guys from the bad guys, and quickly neutralizing any threats through accurate use of weapons. It also included running from point to point and shooting at targets. That's a lot different than standing on the firing line and shooting at a stationary target. Running gets the heart beating and requires focus and control to continuously hit the target. It's a good and logical part of firearms training.

Time and time again, people will react in stressful situations the way they are trained. That's why first-rate training for law enforcement is so important. It's why the Secret Service agents are so good at what they do; their reactions are ingrained from repetitive training. I found on several SWAT raids and other arrests in which I participated that the recurring training paid off, as we were capable of securing a good-size home containing bad guys and weapons in very short order, exercising that good tactical training and the element of surprise. Of course, even the best training and best planning does not always result in a peaceful solution. Sometimes, even when faced with overwhelming firepower, people will still fight. When that happens, the SWAT team is trained to neutralize the threat with minimal risk to the SWAT team members and innocent people present.

Once, we were waiting for the green light to hit a home in Houston where gang members were alleged to be holding the mother and young brother of a rival gang member for ransom. Our staging area was logically chosen to be near to the target home and not visible to the public. In this particular case, we staged in the back area of a huge Houston cemetery. Many trees secluded the memorial park, and the area chosen could not be seen from any nearby public roadways. It was midmorning, and the eight or so of us were dressed head-to-toe in black and armed with our SWAT weapons. We were seated in a grassy area awaiting the word to move when slowly down the path came a funeral procession. I can only imagine what the mourners thought as they drove by and saw eight men, uniformly dressed in black with "FBI" emblazoned on their chests, all standing in reverence with weapons in hand as the funeral procession passed. Within a few minutes, the funeral Director was back with sandwiches and soft drinks to share with us. He was not at all perplexed. I guess we may not have been the first SWAT team that staged in his cemetery.

Subsequently, we got the word to hit the house, a small two-bedroom ranch. One of our guys broke open the front door with a ram, and we entered. I was the second agent through the door and observed the two victims gagged and tied, sitting on a couch, and their captor rising from an easy chair. As we entered, the captor took two steps towards his weapon, which lay on a counter across the room. Seeing us, and probably being relieved to recognize we were the FBI and not some rival gang members, he froze and surrendered without incident. Ultimately, the rest of the kidnapers were caught, and the family was reunited. Our success in this and other situations was attributable to the repetitive and intense training SWAT teams undergo.

CHAPTER SEVEN

MY FAVORITE BANK ROBBERY

I responded with a number of agents and Houston Police to an armed bank robbery one late afternoon and found the bank had been taken for about $225,000. That was a very unusual bank robbery, as most bank robbers walk away with only a few thousand dollars. (It's much safer to get a job in the bank and steal from them internally. When you're caught, and the chances are you will be, you'll do less jail time than a bank robber.)

Towards closing time on the day of the robbery, a senior teller had moved from teller to teller to collect cash and, as usual, was taking it downstairs to the vault, accompanied by a new teller, AJ. After walking the senior teller downstairs to the vault area, AJ excused himself and boarded an elevator to go back to the main floor. The senior teller thought that unusual, as AJ had previously spoken of being uncomfortable in elevators. Immediately after AJ left her, she came around a corner and found a man with his face partially covered waiting for her with a handgun. The senior teller was promptly relieved of about $225,000 cash in her possession, and the young man fled.

While interviewing tellers, I noticed AJ was a very well dressed young man, well spoken, and just a little too sure of himself. Between his actions just before the robbery and his demeanor, I couldn't help but take a closer look at him.

In doing research on AJ, I found that his previous employment had been with The Men's Club, a high-end gentlemen's club in Houston, famous for being the home of future Playboy Playmates and Penthouse Pets. I visited The Men's Club to learn of the teller's employment there. In fact, I visited several times, of course always in the line of duty.

When I approached the manager at The Men's Club, he immediately knew whom I was talking about and told me that AJ had worked as a teller at the club, acting as a cashier for the waitresses and dancers. He had been fired from his job when it was discovered that he had skillfully compromised the security features of The Men's Club's computer-based accounting system and had pilfered more than $10,000. I asked why he hadn't been prosecuted for felony theft and was told by the manager that the District Attorney's Office did not like The Men's Club and would not take on such a case.

Now knowing that I was dealing with an intelligent thief, I tried to figure out the best way to approach AJ. In thinking about an approach, I remembered how well dressed and groomed AJ appeared and surmised that he enjoyed shopping for nice clothes. It also seemed logical that AJ might have spent some of the bank robbery money on new purchases. I started visiting clothing stores within a few miles of his home, armed with AJ's photo. I hit pay dirt at a Kuppenheimers clothing store, which was the third or fourth store I visited. One of the sales managers recognized AJ's photo and was able to pull up records showing that, the night after the bank robbery, AJ had spent several hundred dollars in cash buying new clothes. The fact that he had spent a large amount of cash made him seem a likely accomplice in the robbery, but it wasn't proof. I decided to play a little trick on AJ and see if he would take the bait.

I sat AJ down and told him that, unbeknownst to the public, a program which I named the Bank Robbery Apprehension Team, or BRAT, existed, sponsored by the FBI and the Federal Reserve Bank, wherein for seventy-two hours after cash was delivered to member banks, the serial numbers of the bills provided to the banks were maintained for quick retrieval in a database. Additionally, I informed him that nationwide merchants, such as Kuppenheimers, participated in the program to assist in bank robbery investigations. Under that program, any time a bank robbery occurred, merchants within a ten-mile radius of the bank received a fax from the Federal Reserve with the serial numbers of the bills stolen.

I then advised AJ that Kuppenheimers had called and told me that he had used recorded stolen bills to purchase clothing at Kuppenheimers the night after the robbery. (I described the bills as coming from the Federal Reserve's "BRAT Pack," but AJ clearly didn't catch my jest.)

AJ took just a moment to think about it and then without hesitation stated that his friend must have robbed the bank, as that same friend had paid him a couple thousand dollars he owed AJ the night of the bank robbery. As much as I then tried to develop rapport, minimize, and rationalize, AJ wasn't buying any of it. That's all he would cop to, but it was enough.

I quickly obtained a warrant for AJ's friend for bank robbery. The New Orleans division tracked the guy down and arrested him while he was hiding at a hotel in the French Quarter. I flew over to visit with AJ's friend in jail and told him of AJ's statement implicating him in the bank robbery. He quickly confessed and implicated AJ as the brains behind the robbery.

Both of them were sentenced to ten years in prison. By now, unless he's committed more crime, AJ has been out of jail for quite a while. I hope he's doing well. He struck me as bright and articulate. I thought, at the time, that he had the potential to do well in life.

CHAPTER EIGHT

LEONARD CAPALDI

The gist of the Leonard Capaldi investigation is captured in this letter from the former United States Attorney in Houston to then FBI Director Louis Freeh. (Full disclosure: The letter from the US Attorney was actually written by Ed Gallagher, a senior assistant U.S. attorney, a former FBI agent, and an old friend):

U.S. Department of Justice

United States Attorney
Southern District of Texas

910 Travis Street, Suite 1500
P.O. Box 61129
Houston, Texas 77208-1129

Phone: (713) 567-9000

January 10, 1995

Louis J. Freeh
Director
Federal Bureau of Investigation
Washington, D.C.

Dear Director Freeh:

I wish to bring to your attention the outstanding assistance provided to this office by Federal Bureau of Investigation Special Agent Sam L. Johnson, Houston Division, and Supervisory Special Agent Robert K. Cromwell, Phoenix Division, during the course of the investigation and prosecution of <u>United States v. Leonard Louis Capaldi</u>, Criminal Number H-93-181S.

The <u>Capaldi</u> case involved a joint FBI/IRS investigation into allegations that the defendant, Leonard Capaldi, had executed a complex scheme to defraud individual investors and financial institutions through the sale and subsequent hypothecation of worthless international securities. Capaldi has been linked to the <u>Tocco</u> organized crime family in Detroit, Michigan, and has been a target of several investigations conducted by Organized Crime Strike Forces in both Detroit and Houston dating back to the early 1970's.

Special Agent Cromwell began this investigation in August, 1990, after receiving numerous complaints from Capaldi's victims, several of whom had lost their life's savings to his illicit scheme. After developing a thorough grasp of the many nuances of Capaldi's criminal behavior, Special Agent Cromwell successfully obtained a confession from Timothy Harty, a former Vice-president of Fidelity National Bank, who admitted his role in assisting Capaldi in wrongfully obtaining a series of personal and Small Business Association loans. Mr. Harty subsequently plead guilty to accepting bribes as a bank official, and is scheduled for sentencing January 30, 1995. Special Agent Cromwell's successful interrogation of Mr. Harty and subsequent interviews with several other witnesses led to Capaldi's indictment in November, 1993.

> Agent Cromwell was later promoted to FBI Headquarters and was replaced by Houston Special Agent Sam L. Johnson. Agent Johnson, starting in October, 1992, provided invaluable assistance to the prosecution team. Johnson prepared the case for indictment and trial by assisting the IRS with gathering and organizing an immense quantity of physical and documentary evidence necessary to establish Capaldi's guilt in bribing Mr. Harty and defrauding Fidelity National Bank of assets in excess of $250,000. He dedicated countless hours of personal time in coordinating conferences and travel for a multitude of witnesses. He also arranged for and assisted with the September, 1993, deposition of a Capaldi accountant at your FBI LEGAT, London, England.
>
> Assistant United States Attorneys Edward Gallagher and Michael Shelby of the Special Prosecutions Division have informed me that these agents played critical roles in bringing this case to a successful conclusion.
>
> Based largely upon the quality of the evidence gathered by Special Agent Cromwell and later organized by Special Agent Johnson, on January 6, 1995, Capaldi entered a plea of guilty to bank fraud and bribery of a bank officer. This plea came moments before jury selection was scheduled to begin before U.S. District Judge Kenneth M. Hoyt.
>
> The guilty plea was a significant accomplishment in that it came from a 61 year-old "con man" who had successfully avoided prosecution from a multitude of jurisdictions for years. Capaldi is scheduled for sentencing before Judge Hoyt on March 27, 1995. Special Agent Johnson continues to assimilate information and evidence relevant to the determination of sentence.
>
> Simply stated, Supervisory Special Agent Robert K. Cromwell, Phoenix Division, and Special Agent Sam L. Johnson, Houston Division, displayed the selfless dedication and extraordinary ability which merit special recognition by the Department of Justice. Please convey my deepest appreciation and that of this office to these fine professionals for a job well done.
>
> Very truly yours,
>
> GAYNELLE GRIFFIN JONES
> United States Attorney
>
> cc: SAC Michael D. Wilson
> Houston Division
>
> SAC Weldon Kennedy
> Phoenix Division

Capaldi was an interesting investigation involving a large number of victims, many who lost their life's savings to the smooth-talking Villain. It was a truly despicable crime, which included taking advantage of the elderly.

One facet of the investigation stays in my mind. Leonard Capaldi was using a scheme to defraud, allegedly perfected by an elder OC character from Detroit whom I'll call "George" (not his real name), who in the late 1980s was living in Canada. George had been in prison in Canada on fraud charges when he was diagnosed with cancer. In Canada at that time, when a non-violent inmate was determined to be sick with a terminal illness, the inmate could appeal to be paroled to home under the supervision of a Hospice service. George was one such person. He had been diagnosed with terminal cancer while in prison and had been sent home to die.

I traveled to a picturesque Canadian resort town to meet George, as I wanted to see if he would provide some insight into the scheme Capaldi was using. When I arrived in Canada, a Detective Sergeant of the Royal Canadian Mounted Police (RCMP) who had previously dealt with George met me. Since George had been paroled because he was allegedly near death, I was expecting to find him bedridden, under hospice care, and I hoped he was capable of speaking and would see no harm in speaking with me. The RCMP Sergeant drove me to George's home and rang the doorbell. George's wife came to the door. George wasn't home. He was playing golf.

The Sergeant and I then drove to a nearby country club where the Sergeant commandeered a golf cart. We then drove the course, looking for George. On the back nine, the Sergeant spotted George and pointed him out. He was making an approach shot to a green from about 100 yards out. He hit the ball well, it landed on the green, and George looked pleased as he hopped into his golf cart. We followed behind and observed him get out of the cart and confidently stroll to the green to putt. He moved well, and one could not tell from looking at him that he was a sick man.

After sinking his putt, George turned and spotted the Sergeant. Immediately, George's walk back to his golf cart became a slow shuffle. His shoulders slouched, and his stomach distended as he stared down at the ground. I couldn't help but smile. When we pulled up to George's cart, the Sergeant said, "Hi, George. How you doing?" He replied, "Not very well Sergeant. Just getting ready to die."

The Sergeant introduced me to George, and I told him why I wanted to speak with him. George seemed quite pleased that the FBI had traveled all the way from Texas to seek his counsel. When I discussed Capaldi's scheme, George was clearly annoyed that someone else was using his wicked plan without him receiving a piece of the action and, with very little prompting and a touch of pride, he provided me with insight into the process that made up the scheme to defraud. It had to do with employing (bribing) an established market maker in the OTC (over the counter) world to list and promote a stock while knowing the stock was of little or no value. The stock was then promoted to prospective investors as a once in a lifetime opportunity. With an exceptional salesman like Leonard Capaldi, the scheme was worth millions. While today I don't remember all the details of the scheme, I'll always remember Louie's comical metamorphosis on the golf course.

CHAPTER NINE
SOME INTERESTING ARRESTS

Not long after arriving in Houston, I was introduced to a Houston gunsmith who was also a part-time deputy U.S. marshal. (He had the badge and i.d. to prove it. I had never heard of a part-time deputy marshal before.) I joined him for lunch that day and found he was friends with police at the local, state, and federal level and was also friends with local judges, one of whom he had recently equipped with a custom, pearl-handled .45, which the judge carried each day under his black robes.

I ran into the gunsmith/deputy marshal from time to time, and I always enjoyed our meetings. One afternoon, he gave me a call and asked me to stop by his gun shop, as he had something to share with me. I drove to his shop and, after a few moments of welcoming conversation, he advised me that a female friend of his had confided that she had a girlfriend who was dating a guy who was on the run from the FBI in California where he was wanted for Embezzlement. I then sought out and spoke with the gunsmith's lady friend, and she explained that the wanted man had convinced his new girlfriend that he had been set up by his two business partners in California and that the FBI was looking for him. His girlfriend was therefore helping him establish a new identity. He was employed as the maître d' at an elegant restaurant and club in Houston.

Another agent and I found the alleged wanted man at his place of employment. He was impeccably dressed, well tanned, and looked as though he could have been fresh off the cover of GQ. After we introduced ourselves, I told the guy that we understood the FBI was looking for him, as he was wanted in California. He was quite articulate and smoothly assured us that there must have been a mistake, and he offered to show us his Texas Drivers License. I advised him that for us to resolve the matter we were going to have to take his fingerprints, and 45 minutes thereafter, we would know who he was. I added that, if he were lying, he would be charged with the felony crime of lying to an FBI agent, punishable by ten years in prison. (True statement. It's a felony to lie to an FBI agent unless, of course, you were one of my three teen-aged sons.) I also informed him that if he was wanted and was honest with us, we would bring the fact of his cooperation to the attention of the prosecutor.

I was bluffing, as we had little justification to detain him long enough to get a fingerprint match. At that time, circa '87-'88, the process of taking his prints, enlarging each one, placing each separate print on one of those old drum fax machines, and then sending them in to the FBI's Identification Division would have taken more than an hour, followed by a several hour wait, if we were lucky, for the Identification Division to hand-search the fugitive prints. We knew we simply could not detain him for that long a time. (Things sure have changed. Prints are now optically scanned, and you can obtain a wanted/not wanted determination in a couple of minutes.)

But, sometimes a bluff works. In this case, he decided to come clean and tell us who he was. We then had the NCIC clerk in our office conduct an NCIC wanted person inquiry and quickly determined that he was, in fact, a wanted man in California.

However, it wasn't for embezzlement.

He was a serial rapist.

He had warrants outstanding in California for multiple counts of kidnapping and rape. When given his rights, he decided he wanted to speak to an attorney, so we verified he was wanted with authorities in California and transported him to the Harris County Jail in downtown Houston where we turned him over to the Harris County Sheriff's Department to be held for California authorities. It was a good day.

You never knew where a fugitive investigation might take you. On one occasion, two other agents and I paid a 5:00 a.m. visit to the home of a Houston Rocket and arrested his friend who was wanted up north for Murder. The player came walking out of his room rubbing his eyes. It was a sight to see. NBA players are often really, really large in person and this guy fit that bill. His shock at learning what we were doing led me to believe he had no idea the trouble his friend was in. Nevertheless, the Rocket's front office was not very happy with that player. I think he may have been traded the following year.

One of the crimes the FBI addresses is interference with child custody, also known as parental kidnapping. When a parent takes a child from the other parent and runs away without proper custody agreements, a local arrest warrant for parental kidnapping is often issued. Once that warrant is issued, if the local investigators determine a likelihood that the parent has taken the child across state lines, the FBI can be requested to obtain an unlawful flight warrant and then to locate and arrest the parent and return the child.

One such case I remember well. The subject, a Vietnamese woman married to a US Army veteran, had taken her nine-year-old daughter from a northern state and was thought to be somewhere in Texas. I could find no record of the mother anywhere in Texas. So, with a subpoena for school records in hand, I approached school district administrations seeking the child. I located the child in a Houston elementary school. After explaining the issues to the school principal, the principal told me that the child was a gifted student who got along well with other students and was doing exceptionally well in her new school.

The school had an address for the child's home that turned out to be no good.

The next day, after obtaining the child's photo from the principal, I waited on a side street near the school and observed the child walk out of the school and head down the street. I followed from a distance and observed her arrive at a nearby apartment complex and walk up the stairs and into a second floor apartment. After a short time, the child and her mother walked out of the apartment. I intercepted them at the bottom of the stairs.

The mother and child began to cry. We sat down to discuss the situation. While the mother had difficulty with English, the nine-year-old child was quite articulate. The child told me that she and her mother had been forced to run as her father had been regularly beating her mother. The child then asked me, "Have you ever seen 'The

Burning Bed'?" I told her I had. The child stated, "That's something my mother could identify with." For those not familiar, The Burning Bed was a 1984 TV movie, based on a true story, about an abused woman who set her bed on fire and killed her husband. The precocious child also told me that her father "had money" and was getting away with abusing her mother.

The child was incredibly convincing, and I believed her. Here I was, about to place the mother in jail and ultimately send the child back to a potentially horrendous situation. I decided to see what I could do to help.

The federal government has a system of public defense attorneys who are federal employees. I ran into them from time to time in federal court and knew a couple of them to say hello to. One, who struck me as a decent person and good attorney, was Mike Wallace. I contacted Mike the same day I arrested the woman and explained the situation. Mike then really came through. Not only did Mike represent the woman in Houston, but he also, through his contacts, obtained competent representation for her in her home state. He went the extra mile for the poor lady, and I really appreciated it. I never heard the outcome of the case from up north, but I know that Mike Wallace and I did what we could do in Houston to help the woman and her child get a fair chance in the justice system. (In case you were not aware, the justice system isn't always fair. I've borne witness to that fact on several occasions.)

CHAPTER TEN

SPECIAL AGENT PHIL STUKES

Phil Stukes was with me on many arrests. Besides being a great guy, he was a solid, dependable agent with whom I enjoyed working. Phil is also African American. That fact led to a couple of interesting events.

Once, Phil and I were out with a brand new agent, also an African American, giving the new agent an arrest experience in downtown Houston. A fugitive wanted for assault on a police officer was walking from a Houston business, and we pulled up in our car to take him into custody. He cooperated with us without a problem and admitted his identity. Normally, we would have taken him off the street quickly and been on our way, but he had a friend with him, on who we needed to run NCIC wanted-person inquiries. So we handcuffed both men, and while Phil and the new agent detained the fugitive and his friend on the sidewalk, I made radio contact with our office to run an NCIC wanted-person inquiry.

As was often the case when making an arrest in downtown Houston, a group of street people gathered to watch. I was waiting for the FBI radio room to get back to me and overheard the conversation between a couple spectators. It went like this:

Male #1: They're HPD. (That would be the Houston Police Department)

Male #2: No way they're HPD. They're Texas Rangers!

Male #1: Don't be stupid. Ain't no way the Texas Rangers got two black Rangers!

He was probably right. The first African American Texas Ranger was appointed in September of 1988, which was right about the time we had this encounter. (And it turned out the guy walking with our fugitive was also wanted.)

On another occasion, while out with Phil and that same new agent, we arrested a white fugitive, processed him, and transported him to the Harris County Jail in downtown Houston. (Last I heard, the Harris County Jail in downtown Houston frequently has a daily inmate population of about 10,000.)

That new African American agent was a sharp dresser. He wore clothes that would not have stood out in New York, Los Angeles, or other northern cities. On this day, he was wearing a well-tailored dark sharkskin suit. He looked good, but I guess it was a suit you did not often see in Texas.

As Phil and I walked in with the white fugitive and the new agent, the deputy behind the counter took one look at the new agent in the sharkskin suit and ordered him to, "Empty your pockets!" Phil and I laughed out loud, but it was a somewhat uncomfortable laugh. It seemed a humorous mistake, but I was sorry the new agent had been the target of stereotyping by the deputy.

I believe it's sometimes not easy being a person of color in law enforcement, dealing with parts of society that judge individuals by the color of their skin. It's a complex problem. I've always thought that having diversity in law enforcement would help address the problem. If a community is 33 percent white, 33 percent Latino, and 33 percent African American, the police department would probably get along better with the community if the police department's racial makeup, and management structure, reflected those percentages.

I've read many accounts of questionable officer-involved shootings of persons of color. It's been characterized by some as a need for more training for police officers. I certainly believe in ongoing and meaningful training. But I've worked with police in many agencies all over the country and I know the rogue officer is a rarity. There are easily over a million traffic stops a day in the U.S., and you never hear about them unless something goes terribly wrong. I hear the argument that something has to be done with out-of-control police. Well, the number of "out-of-control" police is very, very low and does not reflect the behavior of the vast majority of police officers. The public needs to recognize that and also recognize and appreciate that police officers work around the clock to maintain a safe environment for their communities.

That said, the dual standard by which different members of society are addressed should be continuously examined. Training must be ongoing and meaningful. It's not always a matter of the person's color. It's often the person's economic situation that changes how the person is approached and handled by police officers. In my experience, double standards exist and most often reflect economic differences in the community.

The people in poor economic situations need to see the police as more than just enforcers of the law. They need to see the police as public servants, helping their communities be safe. That requires the police to not only enforce the law, but to also have meaningful, non-enforcement contact with the community. That's often called community policing. As the police and the public they serve get to know one another, a two-way channel of trust and understanding can be developed. That leads to more efficient policing, better community relations, and lower crime rates. Of course, what I describe presupposes that the police department has sufficient officers to allow them to take the time to get to know their communities. Understaffed police departments have a difficult if not impossible task in addressing community policing. You can't take the time to get to know the community if, all shift long, you're running from one 911 call to another. Community policing doesn't work without sufficient personnel in the department. That requires funding. It's money well spent.

CHAPTER ELEVEN

MARCUS HAMILTON
UFAP - CAPITAL MURDER

New Year's Eve in Texas, as in many states, is celebrated with fireworks. We had a tradition at our house in Texas of putting on a pretty decent fireworks display, with large bottle rockets and oversized mortar shells. On New Year's Eve, 1987, we had several neighbors over at the house for a cookout and fireworks. It's a New Year's Eve I'll always remember. The cookout had to start without me since I was quite late coming home.

Saint Joseph's Society of the Sacred Heart, known as the Josephites, are a community of Roman Catholic priests founded in Mill Hill, England, in 1866. In 1871, four Mill Hill priests came to the United States to work with freed slaves. Then, in 1893, the American community of Josephites separated from their English counterparts, forming two independent entities. The Josephites in America were established to serve black Catholics in the Deep South to allow them to worship freely without feeling segregated. That segregation was often seen in churches that only allowed black churchgoers to sit in the balconies. The Josephites provided churches where the black parishioners could sit and worship anywhere they pleased.

Father Patrick McCarthy was one such dedicated Josephite priest. He worked as the Pastor of an urban New Orleans church, tending to the needs of a predominantly African American parish. To this day, I often think of and am disturbed by Father McCarthy's death.

Around December 10, 1987, ex-con Marcus Hamilton was introduced by his half-brother, Bernard Joseph, to Father McCarthy. Having no place to stay, Hamilton sought shelter at the church and was given a temporary place to stay in the rectory. During the eight days Hamilton stayed at the rectory, the church secretary became alarmed by

Hamilton's demeanor and told Father McCarthy that she was afraid of Hamilton. After consulting with another Catholic priest who knew Hamilton and his family, Father McCarthy decided Hamilton had to move out of the rectory and told him he had to be out by Friday, December 18.

On the morning of December 18, staff members found Father McCarthy dead on the floor of the rectory. He was dressed in a robe and was bound hand and foot with pieces of electrical cord. Another cord was wrapped around his neck.

Investigation in New Orleans by the police and medical examiner ultimately determined the order of assault on Father McCarthy. He was first hit in the head/skull with a hammer-like object, and then he was bound and tied. Thereafter, an extension cord was wrapped around his neck, and he was stabbed several times in the throat. Next, salt was poured down Father McCarthy's throat. Finally, he was strangled with the extension cord wrapped around his neck, which ultimately caused his death. Salt had also been poured on Father McCarthy's eyes.

Police determined Hamilton was gone, along with the parish's vehicle, an unknown amount of cash, a television, a VCR, and a carpenter's hammer. Hamilton's fingerprints were found on a drinking glass in Father McCarthy's bathroom, a strongbox on Father McCarthy's desk, and on a drinking glass from another bedroom.

Subsequently, the New Orleans Police Department requested that the FBI in New Orleans obtain an arrest warrant for unlawful flight to avoid prosecution for first-degree murder for Marcus Hamilton.

On the afternoon of December 31, 1987, following leads provided to us by the New Orleans office, Agents Phil Stukes, Andy Tully, and I traveled to Baytown, Texas. Baytown is a city on I-10 about 30 miles east of Houston, and based on our leads, we believed that Hamilton was visiting an apartment complex there.

Upon arriving, we observed Father McCarthy's stolen Chevy Blazer parked in a covered parking area. The apartment where Marcus was thought to be staying was an end unit.

There was construction taking place in the immediate area, so Phil Stukes donned my Southwestern Bell telephone company hardhat and went to the door of the apartment with a clipboard and pen in hand while Andy Tully and I hid just around the corner from the door with our backs up against the brick sidewall. Marcus Hamilton opened the door, Phil greeted Hamilton, and I spun around the corner and pointed my pistol in Hamilton's face. He did not resist.

After Hamilton was cuffed, Phil and I transported him to the FBI office in Houston. We sat down with Marcus in an interview room and started to talk. He stated that he understood his rights and signed an Advice of Rights form, and indicated that he was willing to speak with us. After some preliminary chatter, I told Marcus, "You know, Father McCarthy is dead; God knows what those cops in New Orleans are going to say about you. This is a good opportunity for you to get your side of the story on the record. You know the FBI doesn't lie. We will only report what you tell us. You might not get a chance to talk to the FBI again."

I know I was demeaning the New Orleans police, but as Hamilton was someone with a long history in the criminal justice system, it was a safe bet that he didn't like the police, and in order to establish rapport, it made sense to take that tack. It seemed, at least partially, to work, as Marcus quickly admitted taking Father McCarthy's Chevrolet Blazer. However, Marcus claimed that he hadn't killed Father McCarthy, and he stayed with that story for some time.

We worked to develop good rapport with him; we treated him with courtesy and respect and tried to show him that we were interested in him and that we enjoyed speaking with him. But, he continued to insist he hadn't hurt Father McCarthy. He was not going for the murder. While I spoke with Marcus, I looked hard for something that I might use to help him hang his hat on with respect to rationalizing what he'd done to Father McCarthy.

I decided on the spur of the moment to imply that Father McCarthy had made inappropriate advances and had provoked Marcus's violent reaction, to see if Marcus would take the bait. I told Marcus, "I figure that Father McCarthy was coming on to you and you just lost control." That thought seemed to immediately appeal to Marcus. You could see it in his eyes. He quickly considered it and decided that blaming the crime on the priest's actions made sense. I would bet that Father McCarthy never made advances of a sexual nature towards Marcus Hamilton. But it was clear that, after thinking about it for a moment, my rationalization sounded good to Marcus, so he decided to run with it. It subsequently became part of his basis for appeal, which also included the claim that he had allegedly been abused by priests as a young man, although that might have been the work of an inventive defense attorney trying to keep his client off death row.

After grabbing onto an "excuse" for his actions, Hamilton gave details. He stated, "That priest put his hands on me every time I got near him." He also said that Father McCarthy kept asking him to sleep in the priest's room. According to Hamilton, on December 17th, his brother Bernard Joseph and Father McCarthy had dinner with Hamilton. After dinner, Father McCarthy went to bed. Hamilton stated that he told his brother that if the priest did not leave him alone, he would "have to hurt him, and if I hurt him, I would have to kill him."

After dinner, Hamilton brought the rectory keys to Father McCarthy, and Father McCarthy again "came on" to him. Hamilton stated, "Right then and there, I knew I was going to hurt that man." He then began hitting Father Hamilton with a hammer he had conveniently brought to the room with him. Although Hamilton hit Father McCarthy "hard," he did not pass out but just rolled out of the bed, said that he was cold, and asked for his robe. Hamilton claimed that, at that point, he thought he would just "knock Father McCarthy out" and take his vehicle.

By then Hamilton's brother Bernard Joseph had rejoined Hamilton. They located about $80 in one dollar bills and "thought of just leaving," but decided Father McCarthy would call the police to report the robbery. So Hamilton and Joseph "decided the easiest way out of it would be to choke him." Hamilton stated they then found an extension cord, wrapped it twice around Father McCarthy's neck, and "pulled hard for a long time," perhaps ten minutes. When they stopped pulling, Father McCarthy was "still trying to breathe." So, according to Hamilton, his brother then stabbed Father McCarthy four times in the throat. Then they pulled on the ends of the extension cord "really hard for about fifteen minutes." Bernard Joseph then poured salt on Father McCarthy (including down his throat). When they concluded that Father McCarthy was dead, they "took some things" and left in the parish's vehicle.

The idea that being approached by a gay priest would justify assault and murder is appalling, but Phil and I had to keep that to ourselves and continue to befriend Marcus. We wanted to obtain the whole story from Marcus, and we ultimately did. It's interesting, and calls to question the "gay" component of the confession, that Hamilton chose to attack Father McCarthy only after being told that he had to move out of the rectory. Being forced to depart the rectory, in all likelihood, is why the murder actually occurred. After close to six hours of talking, we obtained a three-page statement that detailed the horrible things Marcus and his brother did to Father McCarthy. With statement in hand, we concluded our interview and put Marcus in the Harris County Jail.

Six hours seems like a long interview. It was. But it was pleasant, and through the entire interview, we treated Marcus with respect. It simply took that long to gather all the details. When interviewing suspects, I always attempted to show respect and worked to develop rapport. It's the best way to get someone to talk. At that time, the Bureau did not allow recording of interviews. I believe that has changed. I have always thought that recording the entire interview is appropriate. That way, the jury can hear the whole story, and allegations of mistreatment of the suspect can be avoided.

Phil and I subsequently testified in Marcus Hamilton's trial in New Orleans. The written confession was admitted into evidence and is quoted in the Louisiana Supreme Court appeal decision, which upheld the death penalty.

After hearing all the evidence and the arguments from the state and defense attorneys, the jury quickly convicted Marcus and ultimately sentenced him to death. When I say quickly, when it came time to determine guilt or innocence, the jury retired at about five p.m., had a fried chicken dinner, and came back at six-thirty p.m. with the guilty verdict. By any standard, that's quick.

The punishment phase, which was like a separate trial and occurred the next day, was a bit different. The jury was out for two hours, came back with a couple of questions for the judge, and then was out for another hour or so. I watched the jurors as they returned to the jury box and noted a couple with tissues in their hands and tears in their eyes. I knew they had returned with the death penalty for Hamilton.

It was also interesting to observe the interaction of the defense attorneys and priests who were present as spectators during the trial. There were five or six priests constantly on hand in the courtroom throughout the proceedings. I watched as the defense attorneys spoke with them individually during breaks in the trial, approaching each priest and asking him what he thought of capital punishment. Each priest had roughly the same reply: "I'm not really sure." If any of the priests had replied that they were against the death penalty, I imagine that the priest would have been called as a witness during the punishment phase of the trial. The Roman Catholic Church may be against the death penalty, but you better not count on their support if you kill a Catholic priest.

Two of the best police shows of all time are *Hill Street Blues* and *NYPD Blue*. Both are very well written, developing each central character well beyond the character's role as a police officer. On Hill Street Blues, the character development was superb. I tried to never miss an episode and have all the episodes on DVD. The show has passed the test of time.

Two of the many great characters on *Hill Street Blues* were Bobby Hill, played by Michael Warren, and Andy Renko, played by Charles Haid. Bobby Hill was an intelligent, sensitive officer who worked diligently to rein in his good friend and partner, Andy Renko. Andy came across as a brash, loud officer who, underneath his harsh demeanor, possessed sensitivity that Bobby recognized and appreciated. The relationship between them was often complicated and rich with conflict on and off the job. Michael Warren and Charles Haid were both great at bringing to life the Hill and Renko characters.

I mention *Hill Street Blues* because it came to be on my mind during Marcus Hamilton's trial. The movie *Storyville*, starring James Spader and co-starring Charlotte Lewis and Jason Robards, also featured Michael Warren and Charles Haid. During Marcus Hamilton's trial, the courtroom directly next to ours was being used as a set for the movie. I think James Spader a great actor, and while I was waiting to be called to testify, I watched him quickly pacing back and forth in the hallway that fronted the courtroom in anticipation of the next scene. It appeared that he was intentionally working up a sweat or state of fervor for the scene that was about to be shot in the courtroom. Perhaps that's a facet of method acting? Whatever it is, it clearly works for Spader.

Anyway, I was called into the courtroom to testify. As I raised my right hand to be sworn in, there, seated in the back of the courtroom, was Michael Warren. I had to smile, and if the judge had asked me why I was smiling, I would have pointed at Michael Warren and told him it was Bobby Hill from *Hill Street Blues*. For me, it was a happy, surreal moment in a deadly serious environment.

I've often wondered if my suggestion of sexual harassment as a motive was the right thing to do. The way Marcus thought about it for a few moments and then lit up and embraced the explanation when offered made me think that Father McCarthy clearly hadn't harassed Marcus and that Father McCarthy had been killed so he couldn't testify against the brothers.

In thinking back on it, I did not know how strong the New Orleans Police Department case was against Marcus and felt justified in offering him an excuse that resulted in his confession. It was likely the right thing to do.

Subsequently, Marcus suffered a stroke in prison, and his sentence was changed to life without the possibility of parole. He resides at the Louisiana State Prison in Angola, Louisiana.

I always appreciated letters from the Director for a job well done, but I especially appreciated the letter sent to my boss at the time, SAC Andrew Duffin, by Father McCarthy's brother, who was an assistant United States attorney in New York:

U.S. Department of Justice

United States Attorney
Western District of New York

620 Federal Building
Rochester, New York 14614

Telephone:
(716) 263-6760
FTS: 963-6760

June 6, 1991

Andrew Duffin
Special Agent in Charge
Federal Bureau of Investigation
2500 East T.C. Jester
Suite 200
Houston, Texas 77008

Re: Marcus Hamilton Trial, New Orleans, LA.

Dear Special Agent Duffin,

Allow me to take a few moments of your time to complement two superb Agents under your command.

In December, 1987, my brother, Josephite Father Patrick McCarthy was the victim of a particularly brutal homicide. Mr. Hamilton fled New Orleans to your jurisdiction.

Special Agents Robert Cromwell and Philip Stukes played the important role of obtaining a statement from Mr. Hamilton. But, as you know, it is the follow-up work on the witness stand that is the most crucial part of law enforcement.

Under vigorous cross-examination both Agents Stukes and Cromwell were the picture of cool, thoughtful professionals. It was obviously to me that their contribution to the case was largely responsible for the Murder 1 conviction of Mr. Hamilton.

Please accept my thanks and that of my entire family for the exceptional work of these two fine men.

Very truly yours,

DENNIS C. VACCO
United States Attorney

By: BRIAN M. McCARTHY

CHAPTER TWELVE

CRIMESTOPPERS

While I was assigned to the Houston Division, the local Crimestoppers program was annually recognized as the most proficient in the world. Since it was established in 1981, Crimestoppers of Houston has helped solve over 30,000 crimes, been responsible for the arrest of over 25,000 felony fugitives, and paid over $10 million in cash rewards. That cash comes from contributions from businesses and individuals.

During my eight years in Houston, HPD Sergeant John Gilbert ran Crimestoppers and was extraordinarily innovative and cooperative in working with all law enforcement agencies in his efforts to locate fugitives. He, and the policies he established, were responsible for many arrests. Crimestoppers occasionally came up with tips on people wanted by the FBI, and I made several arrests based on Crimestoppers tips. It is a prodigious program.

I also participated from time to time on sort of a Crimestoppers ad-hoc task force, led by Lieutenant Tom Frazier of the Harris County District Attorney's Office. Participants included district attorney investigators, Houston police detectives, Harris County sheriff's detectives, a Harris County Precinct Four deputy constable, a deputy U.S. marshal, and sometimes me. When I was subsequently promoted and moved to the Violent Crimes Section at FBIHQ, that Houston task force served as an example to me of how what was to be known as "Safe Streets Violent Crime Task Forces" could successfully function.

I also worked with a few deputy U.S. marshals on several Crimestoppers tips during my time in Houston and found them to be quite good at locating fugitives. Since the events of 9/11, the Marshals Service now conducts many more fugitive investigations. I know that, if I was still working on the street, I wouldn't like that, but there certainly has to be priorities, and many of the UFAP matters have been supplanted by counterterrorism investigations.

During my first couple of years in Houston, I worked frequently with the late Special Agent Andy Tully. Andy was a Houston institution. He had a great, warm sense of humor, and everyone seemed to know and love him. His connections were extraordinary and appeared limitless. His friends included professional athletes, famous musicians, television personalities, wealthy socialites, and con men. He was great at developing intelligence on just about anything imaginable. He was a good friend and asset for many of the new agents in Houston.

Shortly after arriving in Houston, I received a call one night from Andy telling me to meet him at a 7/11 in a Houston north-side neighborhood. Months before, a fugitive serving life for murder had escaped from the Texas Department of Corrections, and a caller to Crimestoppers had reported that he was present at his ex-wife's home in Houston. Andy and I went there with several officers and an assistant district attorney, who carried a badge, was armed, and was a peace officer in Texas. That same assistant district attorney had obtained a search warrant for the home of the fugitive's ex-wife and led the entry into the house. It was quite a production, and until then, I never knew that a prosecutor or assistant district attorney could kick in doors and make arrests; maybe it's a Texas thing. We entered the home to find the fugitive's enraged ex-wife alone in the house. She declared it would be a cold day in Hell when her rotten, SOB, ex-husband was in her house. The call to Crimestoppers was a bust.

After residing comfortably in Mexico for several years, the same fugitive was captured. During subsequent interviews, he pronounced that one of the high points of his time on the run was the night he was in Houston and called Crimestoppers to report that he was at his ex-wife's home. He thoroughly enjoyed being nearby and watching the police swarm into her home.

CHAPTER THIRTEEN
AMERICA'S MOST WANTED

Shortly after *America's Most Wanted* premiered on Sunday nights in 1988, I was able to have a man featured on the show that had shot and almost killed two Houston police officers. After realizing he was the subject of a nationwide manhunt, and partially thanks to the pressure associated with having been featured on *AMW*, the man turned himself in.

In an interesting twist, the man who shot the police officers was verbose in his conversations with his cellmate. The cellmate, looking for some help on his charges, consented to wearing a recorder in the cell. With the recorder running, the subject bragged that his father was very wealthy and had hired him one of the best attorneys in the country and bragged that he was "not going to do any serious time." After the recording was played, the man was sentenced to 99 years. (Had it not been recorded, it would have been one cellmate's word against the other. The testifying cellmate would clearly have an incentive to lie to help his case and his testimony would rightfully be highly questionable. It's an example of why using recorders makes for the best evidence in the criminal justice system.)

With that first success, I was appreciative of *AMW*'s potential. Thereafter, I had a couple of interactions with the show, both as an agent in Houston and as a supervisory special agent in the Violent Crimes Section at FBIHQ. The show was a great asset to law enforcement.

One of the premiere captures highlighted over the years by *AMW* was John Alexander Riccardi, profiled on *AMW* three times. The following is from the *AMW* website, which is no longer on the Internet:

If He Can't Have Her, No One Can

John Riccardi would probably tell you today that he still loves Connie Navarro, the girlfriend he murdered in cold blood.

(Connie was the mother of Rock & Roll Icon Dave Navarro.)

And he would probably tell you, he killed Connie because he loved her so much.

Judging from his pictures taken in the 1980s, Riccardi could have gotten any woman he wanted. But he was attracted to Connie, and she to him.

Theirs was a love affair of opposites. He was from New York; Connie was a California girl.

Riccardi was flashy, flirty, vain, and mysteriously wealthy. He alluded to ties with the mob, but hid the fact he was a common burglar. Connie was fun, hardworking, and an adoring mother to her teenage son David.

What they shared was an interest in bodybuilding and a strong sexual attraction.

If John Riccardi was telling the story, he would say things went sour when Connie decided to leave him. But friends say it was Riccardi's insane jealousy that led to their breakup.

Riccardi couldn't accept losing Connie, so on March 3, 1983, he went to her West LA apartment to talk and eventually kill. Connie wasn't home, so Riccardi, the burglar, broke in and waited, armed with a .38 revolver.

Connie showed up with her best friend, Susan Jory. An argument broke out, and Riccardi shot Connie. She died from a gunshot wound to the chest. When Susan went to help her friend, Riccardi shot her in the head.

That night, John Riccardi began his eight-year-long life-on-the-run.

The Manhunt Begins

In 1983, FBI Agent Ralph DiFonzo had been with the Bureau for 8 years. He was brash, aggressive, and just about the best manhunter in the LA fugitive squad.

When DiFonzo retired 20 years later, he had personally nailed two of the FBI's Top Ten.

But back then, DiFonzo was faced with tracking a not-so-typical murderer on the run. The FBI felt Riccardi's alleged mob ties would help him keep one step ahead of the law, which kept DiFonzo on his toes. From 1983 to 1988, DiFonzo tried to keep Riccardi's face in the news. An ad was placed in Muscle and Fitness Magazine, and the LAPD put Riccardi on their "10 Most Wanted" list.

In 1988, when John Riccardi's father died in New York, DiFonzo requested that undercover FBI agents attend the funeral in an attempt to spot Riccardi.

It was a complete wash. Worse yet, rumors had surfaced that Riccardi had been killed in a car accident and was buried in New York's Potter's Field.

Last Stand for The Ladies Man

In 1989, DiFonzo turned to the new Fox television show, America's Most Wanted, and Riccardi was profiled three times. With each airing, the FBI got closer to their man.

DiFonzo learned from AMW tipsters, that Riccardi was very much alive; he even found the gym where Riccardi worked out in New York. The FBI missed him by days. He also learned Riccardi had had plastic surgery to alter his appearance. But the best clue was that Riccardi had a new girlfriend, a young Scandinavian woman, with a model's looks.

A composite sketch of Riccardi's girlfriend was aired on AMW. A viewer not only identified her, but also provided Agent DiFonzo with information he'd been waiting eight years for: John Riccardi's alias and his address in Houston, Texas.

The End of the Line

John Riccardi was surrounded by 10 FBI agents outside his luxury condominium in Houston. It was January 4, 1991, and his eight years on the run had come to an end.

Riccardi was wanted in LA for the 1983 murder of his ex-girlfriend Connie Navarro and her friend Susan Jory. He had shot them both to death, police believe, using a silencer.

Briefcase Full of Clues

As Riccardi was led away in cuffs, he insisted that the FBI had the wrong man. He said his name was William Failla – a self-employed man who dealt in gold and jewels.

Sure enough, inside his wallet, FBI agents found a driver's license for Bill Failla, but they also found a picture of Connie Navarro, the ex-girlfriend Riccardi had murdered.

But there was an even bigger surprise in Riccardi's briefcase. There, agents found a videotaped copy of his profile on AMW – proving that even fugitives are fans of America's Most Wanted.

Agents also discovered a stockpile of stolen jewelry and cash totaling over $1,000,000. Riccardi hadn't been lying about the self-employed part. He later pled guilty to running an interstate burglary ring. To this date, agents have not identified all the burglaries committed by Riccardi's crew.

After his arrest, Agent Ralph DiFonzo went to see Riccardi at the Harris County Jail in Houston and introduced himself.

"I'm the one who's been tracking you for 8 years," said DiFonzo. "So what," Riccardi replied.

DiFonzo stood up and said to Riccardi, "Well, I'll see ya later, 'cause I'm leaving and you're not."

In early January 1991, I was with several agents conducting a surveillance of an exclusive high-rise condo, thought to be home to Riccardi. (*AMW* says we had ten agents present. I don't think so. We had maybe six working the surveillance.) Another agent and I observed a person who appeared to be Riccardi take off out of the luxury high-rise condominiums in a Cadillac Allante. None of the FBI vehicles had a hope of keeping up with the high-performance Allante, and we didn't want to spook him into running by following too closely, so we tailed him from a distance and waited for him to go back to his condo. When he drove into the condo's garage, I drove my Bureau vehicle into his gated parking garage close behind him, and when he pulled into a parking space, I pulled in behind him. The agent I was with and I jumped out and drew down on him, as a couple of other agents swarmed into the area. He didn't offer any resistance, and he was taken into custody without incident.

An *AMW* production crew arrived in Houston soon after. Several agents had been involved in the arrest, but I ended up speaking to *AMW* and having my interview used on the show. At the time, I had started to look into getting promoted and going to FBIHQ as a supervisor. I told myself that having a TV appearance following a high profile capture wouldn't hurt my chances for promotion. As I look back now, I recognize that I was just showboating because I wanted to see myself on television. (But it's still a keepsake, and I have the video on my computer to remind me how young I used to look.)

Riccardi was convicted of both murders and sentenced to death. Subsequently, on appeal, Riccardi's sentence was changed to life in prison, and he is currently in the custody of the California Department of Corrections, residing at San Quentin.

Regarding the death penalty, I'm against it. First and foremost, our system will not allow the rich to be executed, and often not even convicted of a capital crime. That fact makes the whole system unfair and ignores our nation's concept of "Justice for All." How can we execute the poor while letting the people of means go free?

Also, the system is racist in that the death penalty primarily punishes poor people who kill whites. While homicide victims are six times more likely to be black than white,

77% of death penalty cases involve white victims. As an example, in Florida, a white person has never been sentenced to death for killing a black person.

But a few other things are clear. The death penalty is not a deterrent to violent crime. Year-in, year-out, the southern states have the highest murder rates while also accounting for over 80% of all executions. The northeast and west have the lowest murder rates and hardly anyone is executed in those areas. So, how is the death penalty a deterrent to violent crime? It isn't.

According to the National Registry of Exonerations, of the almost 1,800 exonerations since 1989, 117 of those exonerated had been sentenced to death. God only knows how many innocent people have been executed, but you can be sure there have been many.

I spent a lot of time involved in the Oklahoma City bombing case and I feel that when he was executed, Tim McVeigh got off easy. Being in a "Super-Max" prison, isolated for 23 hours a day, seems a much tougher sentence than being peacefully put to sleep and one I would prefer for him, and others like him, including those who kill police officers.

Bottom line, the Death Penalty is not fair and impartial. It is visited upon people of color in a disproportionate manner. It's visited upon the poor disproportionally, also. It does not lend itself to our country's vision of blind justice. The Death Penalty needs to be abolished.

CHAPTER FOURTEEN

JAMES RANDALL SANDERS
UFAP - ARMED ROBBERY

Among other things, Sanders committed an armed robbery and stole a police car from an Alabama law enforcement officer who had earlier taken him into custody. He had also shot into the vehicle after taking the officer's weapon. Sanders was considered armed and dangerous, suicidal, and homicidal. He had pledged that he would not be taken alive. The case agent tracked him to an apartment complex on Houston's south side. I was one of the agents asked to assist in his arrest. We established a perimeter above, below, and around the second-floor apartment.

I took a position on the left side of the front door and knocked. When a woman came to the door, I grabbed her arm and pulled her out of the apartment, asking her where Sanders was. She immediately advised us that Sanders was in the house with her three young children and several weapons. She added he was high, having just used cocaine. The woman was promptly removed from the area.

As I peered around the doorframe, I could see Sanders standing partway up a flight of stairs, with a gun in one hand, and his other arm held a little girl in front of him. While keeping my weapon trained on his head, I started to negotiate with Sanders from my position of partial cover. Just like I was taught in Hostage Negotiation School, I worked to develop rapport. In no time, we were having a calm, friendly talk, in spite of the terrified young girl standing between us and several armed agents around us. I eventually got around to telling him that we needed him to put down his weapon and come on out. I let him know that the building was surrounded, that he really had no place to go, and assured him that I knew he did not want to hurt the innocent children. He finally began several minutes of give and take over his proposed surrender, asking things like, Should he put the gun down and then let the girl go? Should he let the girl go and then put down the gun?

After voicing various concerns that we would hurt him when he came out, and me assuring him that we would not, he again started to focus on the details of his surrender, going back and forth with various surrender scenarios. After listening to him in his cocaine inspired rant for a couple minutes, I finally said, "James, why don't you just shut the fuck up, put the gun down, and come on out here. We won't hurt you." He promptly did just as I suggested. As James was being taken away, one of the other agents asked me, "Shut the fuck up? They teach you that in hostage negotiation school?" Hey, whatever works.

A search of his home located several weapons, a police uniform, and body armor. Sanders was a good guy to get off the street.

U.S. Department of Justice

Federal Bureau of Investigation

In Reply, Please Refer to
File No.

Houston, Texas
August 23, 1988

Mr. Robert C. Cromwell
Federal Bureau of Investigation
Houston, Texas 77002

Dear Bob,

      On August 17, 1988, you participated in the arrest of James Randall Sanders of the Kings Park Apartment Complex, Houston, Texas. Present at the scene of the arrest were the subject's live-in girlfriend and three young children. Based on the prior knowledge that the subject was armed and dangerous, and described as suicidal and homicidal, you effectively implemented the arrest plan which resulted in the swift apprehension of the subject without incident.

      Each agent in his assigned duties may be called upon to risk their life and participate in a dangerous assignment at a moment's notice. You responded with utmost professionalism to the assignment to assist in Sander's arrest and performed in such a manner that is worthy of special commendation.

      I want you to know that accomplishments such as yours make me proud of the calibre and courage displayed in situations like these by FBI, Houston personnel. You have my special thanks for a job well done.

Sincerely yours,

Andrew J. Duffin
Special Agent in Charge

CHAPTER FIFTEEN

FBIHQ - SAFE STREETS

In January 1992, I was promoted to Supervisory Special Agent (SSA) and assigned to the Violent Crimes Section at FBI Headquarters (FBIHQ), on Pennsylvania Avenue in Washington, DC.

Shortly after arriving there, I was assigned a project with SSA Gary Rohen to establish policies and procedures for the new Safe Streets Violent Crimes Initiative. Gary Rohen was perfect for the job. He had successfully supervised a Newark gang task force, was very smart, and already had a great grasp of how a violent crimes task force should function. It was my good fortune to be teamed with him, and I really learned a lot from Gary. We also had the benefit of two hardworking support people assigned to our project, James Proctor and Jamie Benn. Both contributed long hours and hard work to our success.

The Safe Streets Violent Crimes Initiative was designed to allow the special agent in charge of each of the 56 FBI field offices to establish FBI funded, proactive task forces. The Safe Streets Initiative focused on violent gangs, crimes of violence, and the apprehension of violent fugitives.

Those task forces brought together FBI Agents, local, county, and state police investigators, other federal law enforcement agencies, and state and federal prosecutors to address violent crime throughout the nation. Besides having the benefit of being a force multiplier, the task forces were also able to employ federal laws, such as Continuing Criminal Enterprise Statute (CCE), the Racketeer Influenced and Corrupt Organization Act (RICO), and Unlawful Flight statutes to address the leadership of violent criminal organizations. It also provided the often unheard of sharing of intelligence between the participating agencies.

Since their inception in 1992, the Safe Streets Fugitive Task Forces have been responsible for well over 100,000 arrests. The Gang Task Forces and the other Safe Streets Task Forces have made a significant impact in violent crime reduction throughout the nation. I'm proud to have worked with Gary in forging the policies and procedures for Safe Streets. It's been a very successful program.

CHAPTER SIXTEEN

PHOENIX

After about two years at FBIHQ, having helped to establish Safe Streets Task Forces throughout the nation, I was assigned to the Phoenix division and arrived there in 1994 as SSA of a squad handling crime on government reservations and civil rights violations.

Arizona is the home of 22 Native American reservations/communities with a total Native American population of over 300,000. While I was there, the agents working those communities had their hands full with violent crime investigations. I don't recall the exact statistics, but I remember that, within the State of Arizona, we averaged at least one homicide or sexual assault involving Native Americans per week. It was a busy time, but I had the benefit of supervising a team of seasoned agents who did great work solving violent crimes affecting the Native American communities. I also observed great work being performed by FBI agents in concert with tribal police and several investigators from the Bureau of Indian Affairs.

Hours after the Oklahoma City bombing on April 19, 1995, I was directed to Kingman, Arizona, to help set up a command post. Oklahoma City bomber Tim McVeigh lived in Kingman prior to the bombing, and there was significant investigative work to be conducted in the Kingman area. The initial response to Kingman was impressive. We had several supervisors, a couple of ASACs, three assistant U.S. attorneys, and two SACs on hand, along with a large contingency of FBI, ATF, state, and local officers. However, after the first month or so, things calmed down, and I was ordered to remain in Kingman as the lone supervisor with a cadre of about twenty agents and ten support personnel. We spent close to four months there.

Michael Fortier was our primary focus. He, Terry Nichols, and Timothy McVeigh were in the Army together, and McVeigh lived and worked with Fortier for a time in Kingman. Initially after the bombing, Fortier came across as if he thought he was some sort of celebrity and actually seemed like he was enjoying all the attention. That didn't last long. Ultimately, he admitted to having helped McVeigh move and sell stolen guns, and he also admitted to having visited the Murrah Federal Building in Oklahoma City with McVeigh a few months before the attack. At McVeigh and Nichol's trials, Michael Fortier testified for the government and took a plea bargain wherein he was sentenced to 12 years in federal prison.

Another supervisor and I interviewed Fortier shortly after the bombing, but we had nothing to do with the interview where Michael "gave it up" and agreed to cooperate. That interview was conducted in Oklahoma. I did speak with his parents on a couple occasions and, in seeking their cooperation, tried to convince them that their son was involved in what, at the time, was the worst act of terrorism ever to occur on U.S. soil. One night, near midnight, and a day or so before Michael agreed to cooperate, I was called by his parents and asked to come see them at their home. I ended up sitting with Mr. and Mrs. Fortier for a couple of hours, talking to them, in hopes that they would influence their son to cooperate. I don't know if, in the end, our conversations helped or not, but I walked away pretty sure of having convinced them that their son was involved.

I sympathized with their terrible situation. They were devastated, and it appeared the strain was almost overwhelming. They may have blamed themselves for Michael's involvement, but I knew from the many cases I had worked that bad things are sometimes done by kids coming from good families. In fact, the Fortier's other son was an Army officer and someone of whom they were justifiably proud.

During the first month in Kingman, the ATF had a good-sized group of agents working with us. After I had been in Kingman for a couple months and the ATF agents were long gone, an ATF supervisor, who had worked with us during those first few weeks, called me from his office in Tucson, more than 300 miles away. He told me that they had developed information that an armed fugitive, wanted by the ATF for manufacturing illegal machine guns, was going to be visiting a pawnshop in Kingman that afternoon. The closest ATF agents were more than a 100 miles away in Las Vegas, so he asked me if we could locate and arrest the fugitive for them at the pawnshop. I replied that we would be happy to.

The majority of my time in Kingman was spent reviewing the work of others and insuring that all leads were appropriately covered, but I decided to go out and grab the ATF fugitive myself. It sounded like a nice break from being deskbound. SA Jason Deaton and I went to the pawnshop, and we introduced ourselves to the pawnshop owner. In discussing things with the owner, I asked him if he knew McVeigh. He did not. However, he had met Michael Fortier and added that he had just purchased a rifle from a friend of Fortier's. That information caught my attention. We asked to see the rifle. The pawnshop owner brought it out, and we were quickly able to determine by the gun's serial number that it was one of the weapons stolen by Tim McVeigh during a robbery in the Midwest prior to the Oklahoma City bombing.

Meanwhile, the ATF fugitive came walking in, and we arrested him without a problem. It turned out to be a pretty decent day. We nailed the ATF fugitive and, as a bonus, recovered one of the highly sought-after weapons McVeigh had stolen to help finance the bombing.

CHAPTER SEVENTEEN

JDIG

The Phoenix Joint Drug Intelligence Group, or JDIG, had more than 30 members, with representatives from several police departments, the sheriff's department, DEA, INS, Customs, and the IRS. (INS and Customs are now combined into the Immigration and Customs Enforcement agency, aka, ICE.) Additionally, there was a cadre of FBI and other agency analysts working on the JDIG. After 18 months as SSA of the Crime on Government Reservation and Civil Rights Squad, which included nearly four months in Kingman, I was made the leader of the JDIG.

The common denominator on the JDIG was quality informants. The agents/officers were all good, experienced, and shared the quality of having a knack for working with informants. They all possessed that ability to develop rapport that is so important in the law enforcement business. Working in concert with the analysts, the beginnings of significant drug cases were put together and then disbursed in a ready-made package to participating agencies. Besides providing us with great investigators, many of the participating agencies also provided us with some of their best analysts.

During my tenure as its supervisor, the JDIG was responsible for tons of cocaine and other drug seizures. One case alone resulted in the seizure of ten metric tons of cocaine on a ship in the Caribbean. Another netted two tons of coke out of a Canadian warehouse. While there was a healthy competition amongst the officers/agents, the cooperation was remarkable. Significant cases were spawned by the JDIG for offices and agencies all over the country.

I've had occasions to speak with a couple of formerly successful international drug dealers. They told me that if we (law enforcement) took nine out of ten of their big shipments, they would still be rich, explaining that the drug couriers, boats, and planes they used were "disposable" and success in the interception of large drug loads simply caused the price of drugs to increase. It's certainly something to consider. If there's a demand, there's going to be a supply. Non-criminal interdiction and treatment for users, which would cost the user, and society, so much less than the offender's trip through the criminal justice system, is in order.

U.S. street interdictions overwhelmingly account for most drug arrests. The majority of those snared are poor and often people of color. The larger cities, with large areas of poverty, spawn drug users and dealers who are on the street and more visible than suburban users. Dealers, who are "uptown," or living in the suburbs, are tougher targets for law enforcement. Those same cities have limited resources and often go after the "low hanging fruit" that makes up the street users and dealers. This is understandable, as the dealers out in the suburbs aren't nearly as associated with violence as their inner city brethren and they infrequently interact with law enforcement, but it also accounts for a disproportionate number of users who are poor being arrested.

Middle and upper-class kids, mostly white, are using just as much or more drugs than their inner-city contemporaries, but they're sheltered and considerably less likely to be caught. Furthermore, if arrested, they frequently have the resources to bring in first-rate (paid) legal representation, resulting in pre-trial interventions or other non-criminal-record outcomes. Moreover, they can often afford private drug treatment not available to youths of lower socio-economic status, which is often an incentive for the judge to allow the offender to avail him or herself of pre-trial intervention opportunities.

The result is a disproportionate flood of poor, non-violent people of color going to prison and, consequently, suffering the stigma of having a felony conviction for the rest of their lives.

Violent offenders need to go to jail. Non-violent drug offenders do not. It's not in our country's best interest to jail thousands of non-violent drug users and dealers with violent felons. That results in non-violent drug offenders returning to the street with felony records and effectively excluded from the majority of benefits available to mainstream America. They also often return with prison-acquired violent skills and tendencies. This vicious cycle begets more crime and costs millions and millions of taxpayer's dollars. The only beneficiaries are the owners of private prisons, who bask in the flood of those taxpayer's dollars, which you'll find they generously share with many elected officials. What we're doing now is not effective and not fair. There's got to be a better way.

The NY Times published a compelling article by Jesse Wegman, on July 28, 2014, "The Injustice of Marijuana Arrests." The article highlights the racial imbalance in marijuana arrests and is, from my experience, spot on. Read the article at http://nyti.ms/1nTqLTc.

Phoenix Assistant Special Agent in Charge (ASAC) Jack Hunt subsequently left Phoenix to become section chief of the Intelligence Section in the Criminal Division at FBIHQ. After three years in Phoenix and 18 months or so on the JDIG, Jack asked me if I would like to come back to FBIHQ and be the unit chief of the Criminal Intelligence Development Unit. I said yes and applied for the position. I was selected, and we packed up and moved back to Washington.

CHAPTER EIGHTEEN

INTELLIGENCE DEVELOPMENT UNIT

As Chief of the Criminal Intelligence Development Unit, I quickly ascertained we were an FBI program without resources. The strength of any program in the FBI is directly related to the level of its funding, known then as Funded Staffing Level (FSL), it equates to agents, support personnel, and money in the field dedicated to the program. The criminal intelligence side of the FBI in the mid to late '90s had a zero FSL. Without FSL, the program had very little influence and could accomplish little. Section Chief Jack Hunt was way ahead of his time in his vision of the way criminal, including counterterrorism, intelligence handling should ideally function, but he had very little support from senior FBI leaders, who apparently did not recognize the import of trained competent analysts for the Bureau's criminal and counterterrorism cases.

It was really an uphill battle. The Foreign Counterintelligence Division (FCI) side of the FBI was significantly more advanced than the Criminal Division (which included the Counterterrorism Section) when it came to the quality of their analysts. Within the criminal side of the house, the only trained analysts, for the most part, were those working with the Organized Crime Information System (OCIS) and they were focused on organized crime. The FCI Division had long sought out real analysts, analysts with appropriate training and job skills to provide case analysis beyond a mere regurgitation of what was already known.

For reasons I'll never understand, during those times in the late 90's, the FCI Division did little to help the Criminal Division develop training for our analysts, nor share useful training material. There were some exceptions, but for the most part, we were on our own within the FBI. So, we turned to the military and the DEA for help. In 1989, General Colin Powel established Joint Task Force 6 in Fort Bliss, Texas. (It was initially a counter-drug operation, but was subsequently renamed Joint Task Force North and in 2004 was given counterterrorism as an additional focus.)

While the FBI did not provide standard training for criminal and counterterrorism analysts before 9/11, JTF6 and the DEA graciously provided limited training for FBI criminal analysts in Miami, El Paso, Los Angeles, and Phoenix. Uniform training for criminal/counterterrorism analysts eluded the FBI until after the events of 9/11.

A good analyst takes the data gathered by an agent and conducts research through numerous government and public sector databases to fill in any intelligence gaps, as well as to validate or condense the data. The analyst then dissects all information with the use of analytic tools and determines if there is actionable intelligence for the agent/officer. Potentially significant investigations should feature an analyst teamed with the case agent from the start. The FCI side of the house had long been accomplishing that.

On the criminal side, we suffered with a legacy of analysts who were good secretaries or clerks who had been promoted to the Intelligence Research Specialist (analyst) position. Many of them were quite competent, but were not trained by the FBI in what was expected from an analyst. The FBI did not then have an academy for analysts, and the new criminal analysts basically worked with the legacy FBI-created systems that were in place. Agents still appreciated them, as, for example, analysts took voluminous phone records and put them in a workable database and did other elementary functions that made the case agent's life easier. However, analysts could have done so much more as they were frequently idle in an analytical sense and were not providing any "added value" information, analysis, or investigative leads.

What we in the Intelligence Section of the Criminal Division wanted was a real career path for analysts that included minimum education standards and minimum training. We wanted an analyst's academy. We wanted to emulate what was successfully done by other agencies, notably the DEA and the Royal Canadian Mounted Police (RCMP). FBI senior management was unreceptive, and I used to think that Jack Hunt had one of the more frustrating jobs in FBIHQ. Ultimately, I feel the attacks on 9/11 demonstrated that people should have listened to Jack. I'm not saying trained analysts would have made the difference in discovering the presence and intentions of the 9/11 terrorists, but we'll never know.

Through the work of some very good analysts and managers, and working with people in the personnel section, core competencies were developed for analysts in an attempt to construct an analyst career path. For validation purposes, we introduced those core competencies to the International Association of Law Enforcement Intelligence Analysts for their review, and IALEIA subsequently validated and adopted them as a standard.

The other thing that was a positive development while I was Chief of CIDU was the development and dissemination of fill-in-the-blank worksheets for developing "target packets" for Racketeering Enterprise Investigations, making manageable what was often considered a complicated process.

In those days, the FBI was infamous for its lack of success in the Information Technology world. We in the Intelligence Section wanted a standard set of analytical tools to be on the desktop of our analysts. When Analyst's Notebook (then a new, cutting edge program, which graphically presented detailed link-analysis in complex cases) was demonstrated for some of our IT people, we were told to forget about using it, as anything it could do, the Criminal Law Enforcement Application (CLEA) would also be able to accomplish. CLEA was an FBI homegrown program. Of course, CLEA never did live up to its promise, and years later, the FBI ended up buying Analyst's Notebook for millions of dollars more than what we could have had it for when it was first introduced.

For years, the FBI had been an organization with a vertical reporting structure and a vertical flow of information. For the Bureau to function efficiently, to be able to just get to the intelligence that's available, that flow of information had to be made horizontal. Following 9/11, Director Mueller really pushed the Bureau into that mode.

After a fairly frustrating (but informative) two years in the Intelligence Section, and with the support of Jack Hunt and Deputy Director Bob Bryant, I was named the Assistant Special Agent in Charge of the Jackson, Mississippi, Division.

CHAPTER NINETEEN

MISSISSIPPI

Having been born and raised a Yankee in Princeton, New Jersey, going to Jackson, Mississippi, was an interesting experience. If I heard it once, I heard it a hundred times while speaking with folks in the state: "You're not from here, are ya?" However, the majority of the Mississippians I got to know were friendly, and didn't hold it against me that I was a Yankee, and I enjoyed my time there.

I immediately got to work on familiarizing myself with the FBI's business in the state. Between the headquarters office in Jackson and the satellite, or resident agencies, in Gulfport, Pascagoula, Hattiesburg, Columbus, Greenville, Meridian, Tupelo, and Southaven, the FBI had a presence pretty much throughout the state.

As I examined the cases on the various squads throughout the Division, I observed that the Violent Crimes Squad in Jackson had a Safe Streets Task Force that was primarily acting as a warrant squad for the local police. The task force was arresting just about anyone for whom the locals had an arrest warrant. That's a dangerous practice because an FBI agent normally needs to be able to demonstrate a federal nexus to justify involvement in arrests. When I was a new SSA in the Violent Crimes Section at FBIHQ, SSA Gary Rohen and I wrote the initial Safe Streets policies and procedures, which were reviewed by many FBI and DOJ attorneys. I learned well from Gary, an experienced task force supervisor, and knew of what I was speaking.

I put a stop to the local warrant squad. I understood how unhappy I was making the agents on the squad, as they were having an exciting time running out and arresting people on a regular basis, taking criminals off the street, and being recognized by the community for doing a good service. I would have enjoyed it too and would have been angry with the new ASAC for putting a stop to the practice. The fact that making local arrests did not fall within the scope of an FBI agent's job did not seem a concern. The good they were doing was an example of the ends justifying the means. I could see their point, but the practice wouldn't have passed legal muster and could have resulted in significant liability for the agents involved, as well as their supervisors and the Bureau.

The Safe Streets Task Force supervisor was very unhappy that I had modified his fugitive squad's activities to adhere to FBI Safe Streets standards. He told me so on more than one occasion and I appreciated his candid approach to me. But whether or not he's ever come to realize it, I was doing the right thing for him and his squad. The ASAC has the responsibility for the day-to-day operation of the field office, and I was doing my job, and in the long run, keeping the agents out of potential trouble. But I know not everyone saw things that way.

In Mississippi, corruption was one of our primary focuses. The white-collar squad in Jackson did a great job of going after corrupt police officers. In one undercover operation, corrupt officers were paid to protect cocaine shipments running in and out of Jackson. The drug-runners were actually undercover FBI agents. It was a great case, worked jointly by the FBI and the Jackson Police Department's Internal Affairs Unit and several corrupt police officers went to jail.

Integrity
Police Department probe is merited

The agreement between the FBI and the Jackson Police Department to conduct officer integrity checks should do much to squash any perceptions of wrongdoing.

The Linder/Maple study of the department last spring made the shocking revelation that citizens had the perception that 10 percent to 30 percent of the force is corrupt.

Even more disturbing was that 76 percent of 182 officers who responded to a survey for the study said they believed between 1 percent and 25 percent of officers are taking drugs or money from drug dealers.

Even if there were no evidence of police corruption, the fact that officers and citizens share a perception of it is a serious situation, demanding attention. The Council should be commended for taking this action.

It is especially meaningful that the FBI would agree to help the Internal Affairs Division conduct the ongoing investigations and checks into complaints of misconduct.

This should forestall any potential coverup allegations.

Acting Special Agent-in-Charge Robert K. Cromwell deserves citizen thanks for this.

EDITORIAL POLICY

The Clarion-Ledger's editorials represent the newspaper's opinions and not necessarily opinions of individual employees. The editorial policy is set by the newspaper's Editorial Board. Members include: William W. Hinsberger, president and publisher; David Petty, executive editor; David Hampton, editorial director; Daphne Higgins, advertising supervisor; Jim Ewing, editorial writer; Marshall Ramsey, editorial cartoonist; Eric Stringfellow, public editor; and Lisa Davis of Madison, Robert Gibbs of Jackson, Howard McMillan of Jackson and Dr. Sylvia Stewart of Jackson, community members. If you have a question or comment, please contact: David Hampton, (601) 961-7240. FAX: (601) 961-7211.

I note that while police corruption was rightfully a concern, I worked with some outstanding, professional Mississippi police officers during my time in Mississippi. The corrupt officers were a small minority sullying the reputations of the majority of officers who were hard working, honest peace officers, working for some of the lowest salaries offered police in any state in the nation.

On the gulf coast of Mississippi, I couldn't help but be impressed by the Safe Streets Gang Task Force, supervised by Harry Bowen, the Senior Supervisory Resident Agent in Gulfport, and run on a day-to-day basis by extraordinary Special Agent Jerome Lorrain in the Pascagoula Resident Agency. The task force was making numerous gang-related arrests in the gulf coast area, taking apart criminal organizations, and having a real impact on the area's violent gang problem. It was (and likely still is) a prodigious task force.

In north Mississippi, Hal Neilson was the Supervisor of the Oxford Resident Agency (SSRA) and also supervised the offices in Tupelo and Southaven. Hal and a great case agent put together an outstanding corruption operation. With intelligence aplenty concerning corruption on the part of local officials, the FBI opened an undercover beer and pool hall in a small town outside of Oxford. That's right, a beer and pool hall, run by the FBI. The operation quickly bore fruit, as a local politician who wished to install illegal video poker machines almost immediately approached the "owners." We were soon paying bribes to several public officials in the area.

The establishment had a regular Karaoke night contest. It made me laugh when each month I signed a voucher for "Karaoke Prize Money" for the case. The operation was a joint effort with other agencies, including the Mississippi Highway Patrol, who assigned a trooper from south Mississippi to be the establishment's bouncer. His job was crucial, as he was to make sure no one drove out of the place drunk. SSRA Neilson, the case agent, and several other agents and officers toiled long hours to pull off an outstanding undercover case. The operation was a tremendous success, with many convictions and significant asset forfeiture.

For about half of my three years in Mississippi, I was the Acting Special Agent in Charge During that time and following some highly publicized corruption arrests, the late Jim Ingram, a former FBI senior executive, the then Director of Public Safety in Mississippi, and a really good man, invited me to have lunch with him and Mississippi Governor Kirk Fordice (Governor 1992 – 2000). The Governor was a gregarious, interesting man, and he spoke with expertise on several subjects, including his business of building highways and his many travels throughout the world.

The Governor displayed a particular interest in our police and public official corruption cases, recently highlighted in many Mississippi news outlets. We discussed, in general terms, the problems we had encountered, and the types of political and police corruption we addressed. I also mentioned to the governor that I believed police corruption would continue to be a problem as long as police were not paid a fair and competitive salary. He seemed to agree.

Two young black men, dressed formally in white shirts and bowties, who I assumed were trustees in the Mississippi State Prison system, served us an excellent meal. The two young men were standing at parade rest by a sidewall while the Governor and I spoke of corruption, when the Governor suddenly pointed to them and said with a laugh: "You see these two boys? They're convicted murderers…I can trust them." The impression Governor Fordice gave me was that convicted murderers who had become trustees were more trustworthy than many of the politicians and officials the Governor dealt with on a daily basis. I laughed out loud and so did the Governor. It was a lunch I'll not forget.

I also was reminded, while in Mississippi, that the business of justice did not always function on a level playing field. I had one particular African American friend who, in the late '90s, when he was in his early 60s, told me of his experiences growing up in the segregated south. He had many memories of the Klan coming to town from time to time, doing horrible things without consequence, and he felt he lived in a world that simply wasn't just.

I also became friends with Eugene Bryant, then the State President of Mississippi's NAACP. He's since retired and has become an ordained minister, but while I was in

Mississippi, he was not only the President of the NAACP, but also a Revenue Officer for the IRS. Those are two positions that require a good bit of nerve, and Eugene certainly had it. He had a keen sense of justice and shared with me various injustices that he had witnessed or that had come to his attention during his career in Mississippi. I quickly learned that, if Eugene thought something was worthy of investigation, it was likely something the FBI should look into. He was a good friend who provided much appreciated advice.

I thought about my time in Mississippi and issues of innocence recently, when I read of a Mississippi death penalty case where an observation on innocence is articulated in the case of Anthony Doss v. State of Mississippi, Supreme Court of Mississippi No. 2007-CA-00429-SCT.

In Doss, former Mississippi Supreme Court Justice Oliver Diaz Jr. points out something central to the innocence issue: "Innocent men can be, and have been, sentenced to die for crimes they did not commit. In 2008 alone, two men – both black – convicted of murders in Mississippi in the mid-1990s have been exonerated fully by a non-profit group that investigates such injustices. ... Just as a cockroach scurrying across a kitchen floor at night invariably proves the presence of thousands unseen, these cases leave little room for doubt that innocent men, at unknown and terrible moments in our history, have gone unexonerated and been sent baselessly to their deaths."

Justice Diaz's argument is an observation that highlights the undeniable presence of innocent men and women in prison.

There's clearly still work to be done.

Another thing that surprised me as ASAC in Jackson, and later as SAC in Jacksonville, was the reluctance of many agents to conduct interviews of fugitives they arrested. Agents frequently made arrests, processed the person arrested, and turned him/her over to the jail without ever sitting them down and conducting an interview. One of an agent's core competencies is the development of an intelligence base. (At least it was in my day and I imagine it still is.) Every person arrested has the potential of providing good intelligence about something. Arrestees may not want to talk about the crime for which they were arrested, but they still might offer up some good intelligence about other matters if given the chance.

I even had a supervisor go so far as to tell me that by interviewing fugitives, we were "stepping on the toes" of the case agent or detective who obtained the warrant for the person's arrest. Nonsense. No one is in a better position to obtain either a confession or other good information from a fugitive than the arresting agent or officer. By the time the fugitive gets into jail and is processed, the jailhouse lawyers have "counseled" him, and the chances of him talking are slim. Every person arrested should be interviewed for the crime they are arrested for and for any other information of value they may possess. I obtained too many admissions and confessions and, too much worthwhile criminal intelligence information from people I arrrested to ever agree to not interviewing arrested fugitives. It should be taught as a standard operating procedure at Quantico. (Today, maybe it is.)

At the FBI Academy, as a new agent trainee in 1984, the interview training was not that thorough or beneficial. I received better interview training while going through NCIS training. I hear the FBI's has been much improved.

While in Houston, after being in the Bureau about seven years, I attended Interview and Interrogation Instructor School at Quantico, and they really hammered home the principles of a good interview. I especially remember being shown parts of the movie *Cadillac Man*, starring the late Robin Williams. In the movie, Williams is an outrageous Cadillac salesman, who the audience first meets at the beginning of the movie when he stops to help a broken-down hearse in a funeral procession and has the audacity to try to sell the new widow a new Cadillac. Ultimately, the Cadillac dealership where Williams works is hijacked by a jealous lunatic (Tim Robbins), surrounded by NYPD, and Williams, himself a hostage, becomes the self-appointed hostage negotiator. As comical as the movie is, a critical eye can see that the skills Williams's character uses to negotiate with the hostage taker are the same ones taught at the FBI's interview instructor school. It stuck with me and most of the lessons learned concerning hostage negotiation also apply to subject interviews.

It's one of the best skills any law enforcement officer can have: the ability to conduct a good, thorough interview. It's about developing rapport, minimizing the crime, rationalizing the crime, and really listening to the subject to close the deal (getting the confession). And when you retire, you can always go into car sales.

CHAPTER TWENTY

9/11

I was the acting Special Agent in Charge of the FBI in Mississippi on September 11, 2001.

There are 56 field offices in the FBI, covering all 50 states, the District of Columbia, Puerto Rico, other U.S. possessions, and Guam. Prior to 9/11, every FBI field office established its own priorities, based on the crime problems facing the division. Each field office routinely conducted crime surveys to gauge the various problems and establish justification for their crime problem rankings. That completely changed after 9/11.

Robert Mueller had only been Director for a week or so when the terrorists attacked. The job of every Director of the FBI is very demanding. When the terrorists struck on 9/11, Robert Mueller's job as Director became the most demanding of all. He had to change the focus and function of the FBI, a very difficult and demanding task. I believe that he will be remembered in history for the achievement of accomplishing that transition.

Regardless of any faults of the Bureau, no agency in the world is better at addressing a major case and at solving crimes. The FBI is recognized as the premier investigative agency in the world and by any reasonable measure has lived up to that billing. Many police chiefs, superintendents, and Directors throughout the world will confirm that ranking. After 9/11, the FBI had to change its fundamental focus. It was no longer just the premier crime-solving organization; the number one new mission became preventing terrorism. The FBI still had to be the best at its investigative mission, and it still had to address the most significant crime problems facing the nation. In the midst of that sometimes-overwhelming task, the FBI's foremost mission was to address terrorism, to prevent another 9/11. It was not an easy transition. I give Director Mueller a ton of credit for steering such a huge ship as the FBI and setting it on its new course.

To that end, the FBI's priorities at the time of my retirement were:

(continued on next page)

- Counterterrorism
- Counterintelligence
- Cybercrime
- Public Corruption
- Civil Rights
- Combat transnational and national criminal organizations and enterprises
- Combat major white-collar crime
- Combat significant violent crime
- Support federal, state, county, municipal, and international partners
- Upgrade technology to successfully perform the FBI's mission

I've recently seen the FBI's new Mission Statement:

> "As an intelligence-driven and a threat-focused national security organization with both intelligence and law enforcement responsibilities, the mission of the FBI is to protect and defend the United States against terrorist and foreign intelligence threats, to uphold and enforce the criminal laws of the United States, and to provide leadership and criminal justice services to federal, state, municipal, and international agencies and partners."

I believe the FBI's priorities remain the same.

One of the principal obstacles to the FBI's success has been establishing a robust, nationwide intelligence apparatus. Prior to 9/11, for the majority of crimes, criminal intelligence development and collection was often local in nature, sometimes regional, but seldom national or international. Even when addressing organized crime, the data collected in the FBI's Organized Crime Information System (OCIS) was primarily a collection of local information with limited linked analysis, except for that conducted on specific individuals and families, painstakingly put together by case agents and OCIS analysts. When the focus turned to preventing terrorism all that changed.

If you remember what I said about our analyst cadre while I was the Chief of the Intelligence Development Unit, you'll remember that many of our analysts were former secretaries or clerks who had performed well in those positions and had been rewarded for their good work by being promoted to analysts. I believe 9/11 made that practice finally come to an end, although it was a reluctant cessation. Suddenly, the vision that Jack Hunt and I had shared when he was chief of the Criminal Intelligence Section really made sense. Unrecognized until that time by many, it was clear we needed real analysts who were properly educated, trained, and equipped. We also needed to fix our information technology problems. I've heard that it remains a problem in the Bureau, but much has been accomplished. I've also been told that the Bureau is becoming a much more horizontal organization in the way it shares information and that the give and take between the Bureau, other law enforcement agencies, and the rest of the nation's intelligence community has improved markedly.

After 9/11, I heard many complaints asking why the FBI, CIA, and other intelligence gathering agencies were not sharing information prior to the attacks. I was not always privy to the entire global picture, but I know there was a heck of a lot of information being exchanged. I seemed to spend hours a day reviewing such material. However, from my perspective, there was not a central point where all intelligence was coordinated, analyzed, vetted and properly disseminated. One problem has to do with the types of intelligence the different agencies collected. Among other things, the CIA collects intelligence that influences public policy, allowing our political leaders to make informed decisions. The standard of proof or accuracy does not have to be the same as what the FBI traditionally requires. For the most part, the majority of FBI agents had been accustomed to collecting intelligence necessary to establish probable cause and looking to put together material that would be admissible in court. It's like apples and oranges. The logical blending of the two has been a challenging transition.

One component critical to the success the FBI has experienced since 9/11, and there have been many successful moments, was the establishment of Joint Terrorism Task Forces (JTTF) in every field office. The amount of work accomplished since 9/11 is staggering and could not have been completed without the cooperation of the various state, local, and federal agencies working together on those task forces. The establishment of all those task forces was not an easy task, but fortunately, the foundation for many of those task forces was already in place due to the prior establishment of Safe Streets Violent Crime Task Forces throughout the nation, many of which are still functioning.

While in Jackson, after 9/11, we quickly established a command center to prioritize and address terrorism-related leads. It was a busy time, and there were well over a thousand Mississippi leads covered in a short time. In the midst of covering the leads, we worked with state and local officials to insure appropriate plans were in place for potential incidents of terrorism and the handling of weapons of mass destruction. It was a hectic few months.

Because of these new challenges, I took an action that caused some disfavor for me with the troops in Jackson. I spoke with one of our analysts, who had never been formerly trained as an analyst, telling her that I had arranged for her to attend a five-week analyst training school at the National Drug Intelligence Center in Johnstown, Pennsylvania. This employee was very well liked and a hard worker. She did a great job of delivering subpoenas and returning the subpoenaed telephone records to the requesting agents. She was not, however, doing much in the way of real analyst work. She told me, "Mr. Cromwell, if you insist that I go to that school, I'll retire." I told her that she needed to be trained and hoped she would accept the new challenge. She didn't. She retired, and I know many people in the office couldn't understand why I just didn't leave well enough alone.

One of the leads turned into a case involving a large tugboat pushing a dozen barges down the Mississippi River. One afternoon, as a couple of the tugboat's crewmembers were on deck, a low flying crop duster passed over them. They reported that, when they waved, the crop duster sprayed something on them. Immediately, the tug and barges were quarantined. The Coast Guard responded, along with FEMA, the EPA, and the Center for Disease Control. The crew was quarantined and decontaminated. The vessel was examined for foreign substances. None were found. All crop dusters in Mississippi were grounded, and the search began for the pilot in question. He was not easy to find. I think that he probably read about the quarantine and suspected he was the reason every crop duster in the State was grounded. He may have feared for his life.

A lot of legwork by several agents turned the guy up in Arkansas. He had flown crop dusters for more than 20 years, and whenever anyone waved to him, he was in the habit of "blowing smoke" at them. It was a friendly habit. The crop duster had smoke emitters used for measuring a field's wind flow and direction. Until 9/11, it was a harmless way of saying hello. When people waved, he just hit the smoke button for a couple seconds. I doubt he does that anymore. "Blowing smoke" to say hello cost him, or his crop dusting company, a lot of money, as they were charged with the cost of the decontamination and quarantine.

Another "hot" matter came in one morning when two employees of a business took sick after being exposed to a suspicious white powder on their keyboards. Following a quick, thorough investigation, featuring personnel in Hazmat suits and the evacuation of everyone nearby, the suspicious white powder was definitively identified as powdered sugar off Krispy Kreme donuts consumed by the two earlier in the morning. However, just the thought of being exposed to a "suspicious white powder" was enough to make the two employees ill.

There were plenty of serious leads though, and the FBI personnel throughout the state worked long hours to professionally cover all leads and preserve the safety of Mississippi's citizens.

After three busy years in Mississippi, I was promoted by Director Robert Mueller to the FBI's Senior Executive Service and was made Chief of the Applicant Processing Section.

CHAPTER TWENTY-ONE

APPLICANT SECTION

I spent a little more than two years as the chief of the FBI's Applicant Section at FBIHQ in Washington. During that time, I also spent a few months as the acting Deputy Assistant Director of the Administrative Services Division, a job that included serving as the entire Bureau's Personnel Officer. It was interesting and sometimes labor intensive addressing personnel issues for an organization with over 30,000 employees. Every day brought unique personnel situations to address. It was a busy and eye-opening few months.

As chief of the Applicant Section, I led about 500 people in five units: the Recruiting Unit, the Testing Unit, the Special Agent and Support Applicant Unit, the Special Inquiries and General Background Investigation Unit (SPIN Unit), and the Background Investigation Contract Services Unit. As I learned in Houston, the SPIN Unit managed background investigations of individuals who had been nominated by the President for positions requiring Senate confirmation. The SPINs were always high profile and were handled throughout the Bureau with very high priority. Every Monday, I had to insure the director's office was updated on the status of all pending White House appointment investigations. Fortunately for the FBI, and me I had Linda McKetney, an outstanding unit chief, leading the SPIN Unit, and the unit always stayed on top of its game.

The Background Investigation Contract Services (BICS) Unit, competently led by Chief Maurice Hayes, managed the activities of hundreds of retired agents across the country conducting background investigations for the FBI. The majority were retired FBI agents, but retired agents from other agencies, such as the Secret Service, ICE, and NCIS, also handled many investigations. The use of retired agents freed up tens of thousands of agent hours for the FBI, and the retired agents consistently conducted thorough investigations and provided detailed, well-written reports.

After 9/11, the FBI was granted authority to hire over 900 critically skilled special agents. I arrived at FBIHQ shortly after Congress had given that authority to the Bureau. In nine months, we tested over14,000 qualified applicants, interviewed over 4,000 of those tested, and hired 998 new special agents. The intake and initial processing of applications in a timely manner was critical to meeting the hiring goal. In the not too distant past, when an applicant filled out an application to be a special agent, the application was prepared on paper, mailed to FBIHQ, and forwarded for initial screening and vetting to the field office responsible for the area where the applicant was residing. It was cumbersome and time-consuming, as most applicants did not make it past the initial screening.

Unit Chief Joe Bross, Unit Chief Harry Bowen, Supervisor Gwen Hubbard, and the great people in the Applicant Testing and Recruiting Units, working with several other FBI employees and, most importantly, a private vendor, put together an online employment application system that quickly and automatically performed the initial screening of applicants and enabled field offices to directly download the applications of qualified candidates who resided in their territory.

The importance of that automation cannot be overstated. It was absolutely critical to the FBI meeting its hiring goal. As it came on line, Joe Bross was in frequent contact with the private vendor handling the project and was able to tweak the website to best meet their needs. The difference between working with government IT people and the private sector was so very clear to me during those times. When we found a piece of our system online that required modification, we called the vendor, and the modification was addressed with a sense of urgency and accomplished overnight. FBI IT personnel simply did not possess the manpower to be so responsive. The private sector is profit-motivated and does what it has to do to meet its goal.

From my perspective, our major shortfall was not in finding qualified and critically skilled candidates. We had an abundance of them though they were predominately white and male. Our failing was in not finding qualified candidates of other demographic groups, and we were not doing well at recruiting applicants with Arabic and other Middle Eastern language skills.

If you ask 100 nine or ten-year-old white boys if they think that being an FBI agent would be cool, most will say yes. If you ask 100 African American, Asian, Latino, or Middle Eastern American nine or ten-year-old boys, you won't get nearly the same response. The same thing applies to young girls, no matter what their race. Being an FBI special agent is not something that is part of most young women's dreams. These young people typically saw few role models in the FBI who looked like them, or shared their experiences. It's unlikely that the adults in their lives encouraged them to think about becoming an FBI agent.

Director Mueller recognized the importance of diversity in our ranks, and monitored hiring statistics closely. With his support, we conducted numerous recruiting initiatives aimed at women and people of color. While we gave it a good try, the FBI could certainly do better.

Additionally, Director Louis Freeh had the foresight to grow the FBI's overseas presence substantially during his tenure, a move critical to the FBI's success in countering terrorism and addressing other significant matters. With more and more of the FBI's focus on foreign/international matters, the need for diversity within the FBI's agent ranks is greater than ever.

The lack of diversity within the ranks of the FBI represents an operational shortcoming. The widely accepted corporate argument for diversity predicts a more efficient and functional organization when the organization reflects its customer base. That is particularly true when diversity is applied to the jobs with the most public contact, such as sales, customer service, etc. The sales force that reflects the customer base successfully closes more deals, which equates with more profit. The corporate diversity argument is even more critical for the FBI and others in law enforcement.

The FBI's bottom line is not expressed in profit or loss. The FBI's bottom line involves success in preventing terrorist attacks, catching spies, solving major crimes, and saving lives. If the agent population of the FBI more closely matched the racial and cultural makeup of the U.S., the FBI would be better positioned to succeed; there would be more crimes solved, and there would be more success at preventing acts of terrorism.

Consider the basics of the interview: the first thing the investigator must do is develop rapport. In order to do this, it is helpful to be familiar with the person's culture. It also is critical to be able to speak the interviewee's language.

While it is often easier for people of one demographic group to make a meaningful connection with a peer who shares the same background, we would oversimplify the issue if we concluded that this would be all it takes to achieve success. Rather, if the FBI were to have a more proportional representation, the day-to-day interaction between both the agent and support populations would result in the exposure of everyone to the cultural differences of a variety of distinct groups and demonstrate the many similarities between all people, as well. In such a diverse FBI, cultural awareness/familiarity would breed a better and more efficient pool of investigators.

Support from executive management must be unrelenting. The various minority internships sponsored by the Bureau need to be increased and new, and innovative recruiting techniques, borrowed from the private sector, need to be employed. During my tenure, we reached out through several special interest groups representing minority communities, and we employed 15 and 30-second radio spots during drive time on urban radio stations in many cities. We produced billboards featuring diverse special agents, placing them in urban areas throughout the country, and we even used the marketing talents of the New York Times to attempt to reach new, diverse talent.

Additionally, the FBI must continue to reach out to young people. While I was Section Chief, we started a project wherein we visited colleges and universities with significant minority populations and sponsored semester-long marketing classes in which the students developed plans for marketing the FBI on campus, and then did so. That effort introduced the FBI to many individuals who had not previously considered the FBI as a career choice. The program, the brainchild of EdVenture Partners, an Oninda, California company, was spearheaded by then Acting Unit Chief Gwen Hubbard. It is an innovative program, and in the long run, should produce a more diverse agent population.

The import of counterterrorism investigations should in itself drive home the necessity of a more diverse workforce. The issue is so critical that a full-time FBI Diversity Officer position should be created. (If it hasn't been already.) That Diversity Officer should be someone with demonstrated success in the private sector and with knowledge of the cutting-edge methods being used by the corporate world to recruit a dynamic and diverse workforce. And, most importantly, the recruits must be of the same high caliber that the public has come to be expect from the FBI for over 75 years.

One area of focus for the new Diversity Officer would be the relationship the FBI has with members of the Middle Eastern American community. The FBI needs to join with civic leaders within the Middle Eastern communities throughout the U.S. to recruit Middle Eastern Americans into the FBI. That's where the Bureau will find the cultural familiarity and the language specialists the FBI so desperately needs. That's where the seeds can be planted with young Middle Eastern Americans so that, down the road, they may consider a career as an FBI agent or professional support person. Recruiting from these communities would ultimately lead to a greater intelligence base.

The nature of the many investigations following 9/11 caused a rift between the FBI and many in the Muslim community. In most FBI Field Offices, prior to 9/11, there simply wasn't much interaction between the FBI and the Muslim community because, generally speaking, Muslim children are raised in strict homes and seldom are in trouble with the law. When the FBI suddenly had to interact frequently with Muslim communities in the U.S., liaisons in many of those communities were not already established. It was akin to two unknown groups meeting for the first time. Many Muslim Americans became paranoid – sometimes justifiably concerned -- as many other Americans suddenly perceived them as suspects.

While in Mississippi, I saw instances where even being a suspected Muslim could get you in trouble. A Sikh storeowner was threatened and had bricks thrown through his store window because he "looked Muslim." An Israeli college student who had been locked up for an immigration violation was assaulted in jail because he looked like a "terrorist." There was clearly reason for paranoia in people of color who appeared Middle Eastern.

Today, in order to help identify the Muslims in the U.S. who would do harm to our nation, good liaison with the Muslim community must be an ongoing priority.

The FBI's need to be diverse and to be able to develop rapport with all people couldn't be greater.

CHAPTER TWENTY-TWO

SPECIAL AGENT IN CHARGE

In November 2003, having received great support from Assistant Director Mark Bullock and Executive Assistant Director Grant Ashley, Director Mueller appointed me Special Agent in Charge (SAC) of the Jacksonville Division. I had worked hard and had my fair share of success during my 20 years in the Bureau, but I was still amazed to be receiving an appointment to lead one of the Bureau's 56 Field Offices.

The career path that led to the SAC position had required considerable moving around the country for my family and me as I had moved up the managerial ladder. It wasn't always easy on my wife, Rosa, or our three sons. Michael, my oldest son, had to move from Houston to the DC area between his sophomore and junior years in high school. My middle son, Daniel, had to move after his sophomore year from Maryland to Arizona. Johnny, my youngest, had to move from the DC area to Mississippi after his freshman year in high school. Those moves weren't easy. They've all prospered as adults, but I know those high school year moves were rough.

But I sure was happy to be named and quickly tackled a myriad of new challenges. The learning curve wasn't too bad. While observing some of the SACs for whom I worked, I took note of what I considered smart SAC traits. These outstanding SACs, while maintaining command and control over their territory, worked in a collaborative way within the division. They clearly recognized the tremendous talent they had around them and took advantage of that talent when making decisions. As a result, they made informed decisions, which normally resonated well with the troops in the office and were in the best interest of the Bureau. While I wasn't always successful, I tried to emulate them, realizing that I really was surrounded by incredibly talented men and women.

Throughout my two years as SAC, I worked to collaborate, to get out among the people in the office and take advantage of their knowledge and insights. In the end, I had to make the decisions myself, but I always tried to make logical and informed calls.

The Jacksonville Division includes resident agencies (satellite offices) in the Florida communities of Daytona Beach, Ocala, Gainesville, Tallahassee, Fort Walton Beach, Panama City, and Pensacola. Those last three are in the Central Time Zone. While SAC, I also established a one-agent office at the Federal Correctional Complex (FCC) in Coleman, Florida.

FCC Coleman featured two high security prisons, one medium security prison and one low security prison. There's a population of over 7,000 prisoners, making it the largest Federal Bureau of Prisons complexes in the nation. The high-security prison has a few notable inmates, including Boston Organized Crime kingpin Whitey Bulger and Leonard Peltier, who in 1975 brutally murdered Jack Coler and Ron Williams, two FBI agents working at the Pine Ridge Indian Reservation in South Dakota. For those crimes, he's serving two life sentences, plus an additional seven years for armed escape from the U.S. Pen in Lompoc, California.

The SAC position came with a myriad of responsibilities. I oversaw the use of traditional and electronic collection, analysis, and reporting of intelligence information. That included overall management of all investigative programs, with a particular emphasis on counterterrorism and counterintelligence. I also was tasked with developing new partnerships within the public and private sector to enhance the division's cybercrime program, and with enhancing liaison with executive management within federal, state, and local partner agencies to facilitate increased participation in the Joint Terrorism Task Force, the Criminal Enterprise Investigation Task Force (a gang task force), and other investigations of mutual interest. While doing all of that, I also had to ensure that our white-collar crime program was aggressively pursuing health care fraud, insurance fraud, and public corruption initiatives. There were a host of other day-to-day responsibilities. I was a busy man. But I had the benefit of having great people addressing their day-to-day responsibilities.

One indispensable person was my Secretary, Suzy Delpezzo. She always seemed to know exactly what was going on throughout the division, made sure I made deadlines and constantly helped me to prioritize my workload. Suzy really kept me informed and organized, as did then ASAC, now SAC Secretary, Carolyn McCormick. Suzy and

Carolyn shared the traits of knowledge of the Bureau, great communication skills, and great attitudes. I think those traits may be common for SAC's secretaries throughout the FBI.

Jacksonville, like each of the other 55 field offices in the FBI, was home to a Joint Terrorism Task Force. Jacksonville's JTTF was unique in Florida due to its all-inclusive composition.

The Florida Department of Law Enforcement (FDLE) is set up much like the FBI, with SACs and ASACs in each of the FDLE's seven divisions. Each of those seven FDLE divisions hosts a Domestic Security Task Force (DSTF). Established by an executive order of Governor Jeb Bush shortly after 9/11, the purpose of the DSTFs is to coordinate the state's ability to investigate and respond to any terrorist threat or attack within the state, working with federal authorities. The DSTF combines the efforts of major state law enforcement and other emergency response agencies such as fire/rescue and health care organizations. Jacksonville is home to the only JTTF and DSTF combined into one unit. The group works together to conduct terrorism-related investigations. At the time of my retirement, an FBI supervisory special agent headed the task force's day-to-day operation, and the assistant head of the task force was an FDLE supervisor.

All members of the JTTF have Top Secret security clearances, participate in legal, operational, and firearms training together, and work as a team on all investigations. The overall operation, which was my responsibility as SAC, received oversight by an executive board made up of sheriffs, chiefs of police, and the other participating agencies' SACs. It is a cost-effective and logical way to address counterterrorism investigations. It maximizes each agency's limited resources. Agents, officers, and analysts are all privy to the same information, and there is much less chance for items slipping between the cracks.

I went out of my way to promote the benefits and logic of the joint JTTF/DSSTF in my speaking engagements and when meeting with other law enforcement officials, but was nonetheless surprised in the Spring of 2005 when my efforts were recognized in a commendation presented to me by CIA Director Porter Goss in appreciation of my dedication and support to the shared Mission of the FBI and CIA.

It is important that task forces addressing terrorism do not compete with one another. The information must be shared in a timely manner. That has not always been the case with task forces. For instance, often in communities where there are multiple drug task forces, the sharing of information that should occur simply does not. Sometimes, that's the result of information just not reaching the right database; sometimes it has to do with an unhealthy competition between the task forces, where one is trying to better the other. No matter what the reason, not working together and sharing information is a cardinal sin and is still of concern since there are so many different agencies investigating terrorist-related matters. Petty jealousies and professional chauvinism cannot be allowed to get in the way of sharing information that may prevent a attack.

As SAC in Jacksonville, I emphasized the importance of having a strong public corruption intelligence base. Outstanding cooperation between the FBI and FDLE resulted in several great public corruption cases, including the indictment of the head of the Florida Department of Corrections and several of his associates. We also had a prodigious asset forfeiture program, as being able to seize the assets of individuals who commit crimes is one of the best deterrents to crime in the FBI's arsenal. Personnel of the Jacksonville Division, with the assistance of an outstanding asset forfeiture team, went the extra yard to include asset forfeiture as part and parcel of their investigations, and in my last fiscal year on the job (2005), more than $110 million in property and cash was seized for forfeiture in the Jacksonville Division.

The job of the SAC is made much easier when competent assistant special agents in charge are present. I was very fortunate during my tenure as SAC to have very competent ASACs. Nelson Durate was the ASAC I worked with the longest in Jacksonville and he was intelligent, articulate and a real problem solver. It was a pleasure working with him. Just as important to an SAC is having a strong Chief Division Counsel. The CDC is an attorney who reports directly to the SAC and who provides guidance to the office on legal matters. In Jackson, as ASAC and acting SAC, I had Mike Turner as my CDC. As SAC in Jacksonville, I had Mike Perkins. Both were outstanding. On a daily basis, they delivered sound legal advice to the office and provided me with solid guidance on just about every subject imaginable, from questions concerning legal matters to sensitive personnel issues. It was my great fortune to work with such bright, talented, and nice people, and both helped me address a myriad of issues in an understandable and logical manner.

I also had the benefit in Jacksonville of working with one of the best police/sheriffs departments in the nation. Sheriff John Rutherford was one of the most competent law enforcement officers with whom I have ever worked. Their department is the police department for Jacksonville, run by the elected sheriff. Jacksonville is, geographically, the largest city in the Continental United States and the department's performance throughout that huge jurisdiction was admirable.

During my stay in Jacksonville, I also worked with, and got to know, Ken Tucker, the SAC of the local Florida Department of Law Enforcement (FDLE). Ken went on from that position to be a Deputy Commissioner of FDLE and then the Secretary of Corrections for the state of Florida. Ken was a pleasure to work with and a truly professional law enforcement officer.

I retired at the end of 2005 to move to Saint Petersburg so my wife and I could be closer to our three sons and their families. It was not an easy decision; I could have stayed three more years before mandatory retirement, but being near our kids and new grandson won out.

With my time in the Navy, the NCIS, and the FBI, I retired with 31 years of service, and sticking around for another three years would not have made a significant difference in my retirement.

People can be as critical as they want about the FBI. It's healthy for the agency to be questioned. But, as critical as anyone may be, the FBI is still the premier law enforcement agency in the world. The many talented and selfless agents and support personnel of the Bureau certainly make mistakes, but the overall emphasis of just about everyone is to do the right thing. The FBI's motto of "Fidelity," "Bravery," and "Integrity" is something most every agent continues to strive for and the American people are well served by such dedicated men and women. I will be forever proud and thankful to have been part of such a remarkable and outstanding organization.

U.S. Department of Justice

Federal Bureau of Investigation

Office of the Director

Washington, D.C. 20535

November 23, 2005

Mr. Robert K. Cromwell
Special Agent in Charge
Federal Bureau of Investigation
Jacksonville, Florida

Dear Bob:

    It gives me great pleasure to extend best wishes to you on the occasion of your retirement from the FBI. Your many years of dedicated and faithful public service are an exemplary model for all who aspire to a career in law enforcement.

    From the beginning of your FBI career in 1984 to your most recent assignment as the SAC of our Jacksonville Office, you have performed your duties in an exceptional manner and have contributed significantly to the success the Bureau enjoys. You have many reasons to look back with pride on your 30 years of devoted service to the citizens of our Nation through the FBI and the U.S. Navy.

    You will be sorely missed by your many friends and colleagues in the FBI. I join them in extending thanks to Rosa, Michael, Daniel, and John for their support during your career and wishing you continued success and happiness in the years ahead.

Sincerely,

Robert S. Mueller, III
Director

> "INJUSTICE ANYWHERE IS A THREAT TO JUSTICE EVERYWHERE. WE ARE CAUGHT IN AN INESCAPABLE NETWORK OF MUTUALITY, TIED IN A SINGLE GARMENT OF DESTINY. WHATEVER AFFECTS ONE DIRECTLY, AFFECTS ALL INDIRECTLY."
>
> - DR. MARTIN LUTHER KING, JR. ALABAMA 1963

CHAPTER TWENTY-THREE

MY FRIEND, JAMES BAIN

Late on the night of March 4, 1974, a nine-year-old Florida boy was abducted from his home, taken to a nearby field, and raped by an unknown male. The young victim described his assailant as a black man with bushy sideburns who said his name was Jimmy. Even though the victim couldn't see the man's face, the victim's uncle, a local high school official, stated that the child's description of "bushy sideburns" fit James Bain, a local high school student. (Details of the case provided by the Innocence Project of Florida.)

After his uncle mentioned the name, it seems the young victim "adopted" Bain as the rapist. When the police arrived at Bain's house, Bain was found at home with his sister where he had been since around 10:30 p.m., watching television. Although James Bain had an alibi and always maintained his innocence, police arrested him.

After the victim had returned home and described the attacker, the police took him to the police station and presented him with a photo lineup. Bain's photo was included in the lineup, along with four or five other males, only one of whom (Bain) had sideburns. Rather than asking the victim to pick out the photo of his assailant, the police suggestively and improperly instructed him to pick out Bain's photo, and he did. It probably wasn't hard to do, as the victim's uncle had shown him Bain's photo in a high school yearbook!

James Bain was charged with rape, breaking and entering, and kidnapping. In addition to the "eyewitness" identification, the State's case was also based on serology tests on the victim's underwear performed by the FBI, which concluded the semen in the victim's underwear could have come from James Bain. The underwear itself was admitted at trial. A defense expert testified at trial, contrary to the FBI testimony, that the serological results revealed that Bain could not have been the depositor of the semen on the victim's underwear.

Serology testing performed before the trial by the FBI on the victim's underwear verified that the rapist did deposit semen on the victim's underwear, and the FBI saw sperm heads on the underwear. An FBI agent testified that the semen on the underwear was blood group B, that Bain's blood group was AB (with a weak A), and that Bain could not be excluded as the depositor of the semen. Ultimately, DNA results now prove this FBI testimony to be demonstrably false.

At trial, the State's theory of the case was clear: the perpetrator who raped the victim ejaculated, depositing his semen and sperm onto the victim's underwear—and that person was James Bain. The underwear was admitted into evidence at trial by the State solely for this purpose. DNA results now prove that the State's theory, along with the evidence used to prove it, were simply wrong.

Dr. Richard Jones, a defense expert, testified at trial that James Bain's blood group was AB (with a strong A) leading to his conclusion, contrary to the FBI's, that Bain could not have deposited the semen on the victim's underwear. DNA results now prove Dr. Jones's conclusion to be correct.

In addition to the expert testimony presented by Dr. Jones at trial that Bain could not have been the depositor of the semen on the victim's underwear, Bain also had an alibi. He was out with friends earlier in the evening on March 4, 1974, and arrived home around 10:30 p.m. From then until the time police arrived at midnight, Bain was watching TV in the living room with his sister, who verified James presence there. His whereabouts were therefore accounted for during the time of the attack. DNA results now show Bain's alibi to be credible. It apparently never occurred to anyone that Bain, who is in no way mentally challenged, would have been crazy enough to tell the victim his name was Jimmy.

James Bain was convicted on all counts and sentenced to life in prison. James recently mentioned to me that at least he didn't get the death penalty, a potential penalty he had faced at trial.

Subsequent to his conviction, and working from prison on his own, James submitted handwritten motions on four separate occasions seeking DNA testing. Testing was denied each time. James request for testing was denied the fifth time, too, but an appeals court overturned that denial. The Innocence Project of Florida (IPF) became aware of the case and stepped in to assist James and his attorney, and James Bain was finally able to obtain the DNA testing he'd sought for so many years.

The state's attorney agreed to the testing, and it determined that the DNA of the sperm found on the child's underwear worn during the rape excluded James Bain beyond a shadow of a doubt, confirming that someone other than Bain raped the victim.

On December 17, 2009, in a joint order, James Bain was declared actually innocent and released from prison. He walked out of the courthouse with members of his family and his legal team. Immediately upon his release, Bain used a cell phone for the first time in his life to call his mother in Tampa, Florida. He had been convicted in 1974 of rape, breaking and entering, and kidnapping and had been sentenced to life in prison. With his December 2009 exoneration, he was released after having spent more than 35 years in prison for a crime he did not commit.

I've come to know James in the past few years through my affiliation as a board member of the Innocence Project of Florida (www.floridainnocence.org). After going to prison a teenager and getting out a 54-year-old man, James Bain started life anew. He's married, has a child, and is working. He is always cheerful when we meet. Quite frankly, I don't understand his kind demeanor. To me, the anger from being wrongfully incarcerated for 35 years would be very difficult to hide. But James shares his story with others and demonstrates a forgiveness that speaks volumes about his character and faith. He's a good person.

I imagine that telling his story of injustice is good for James on some level, but I know it's good for the people who hear James speak. If you ever hear that James is speaking at an event near you, go see him. He gives a detailed account of his 35-year ordeal. It's shocking, and it's eye opening. Everyone should see it.

And "Jimmy," the actual rapist, has never been found, nor, for that matter, was he even sought during the 35 years James Bain was in prison. And everyone should be aware that, for every innocent person in jail, there's a guilty person out there somewhere who is likely committing more vicious crimes.

CHAPTER TWENTY-FOUR

LESSONS LEARNED

After nearly 30 years in law enforcement, starting as a rookie police officer and ending as the Special Agent in Charge of an FBI Division, I've come to recognize some basic truths. While the percentage of innocent people in prison is in the single digits, that "single digit" represents thousands of people. I've learned that the criminal justice system does not always offer a "level playing field." Our system does not feature "Equal Justice for All." I saw evidence of that everywhere I served.

As a New Jersey police officer, I saw several examples. One of my first eye openers was when I investigated a woman who ran a stop sign and smashed into a car that clearly had the right of way. As I was issuing the driver a ticket for running the stop sign, the driver told me, "You know, I'm good friends with the Mayor." That was a hint as to what was to come.

When I came to court for the driver's appearance, the judge, after being given a detailed, diagramed description of the collision, which clearly placed the liability on the Mayor's friend, acquitted the woman and told me that it appeared to him that I should have given the other driver a ticket. The whole thing cried setup. While this is an example from a relatively small community, it is an example of how the system sometimes works.

As an NCIS agent, I conducted an investigation of a Navy captain who had committed and confessed to a fraud costing the government thousands of dollars. (A captain in the Navy or Coast Guard is the equivalent of a colonel in the Army, Air Force, or Marines. It's a senior position.) The captain was given an "admiral's mast." That's what they called his non-judicial punishment, which is usually referred to in the Navy as a "captain's mast" and in the Army as "office hours." The captain was given a slap on the wrist, with a letter in his personnel file and the requirement that he pay back the government. If the offender had been a junior officer or enlisted man, the crime would have been a slam-dunk court-martial, and the offender would have likely received jail time. In this case, rank really did have its privileges.

While in the FBI, it seemed the political party affiliation of the U.S. Attorney and subject sometimes impacted justice. I once oversaw an investigation into bank fraud on the part of an elected county official. The official bragged to his friend, "the FBI can't touch me," and bragged of his political connections. He was almost correct. The U.S. Attorney's Office declined the investigation with no rational explanation, even after personal appeal all the way to the U.S. Attorney.

Ultimately, a couple of dedicated agents took the case into the offices of the state's attorney, who reviewed the case and agreed to prosecute. The subject escaped trial in federal court, but if he had been a man off the street with no powerful "friends," or had he been a member of the "wrong" political party, the U.S. Attorney's Office would have jumped all over the case. U.S. Attorneys love cases they can take to court with little or no chance of losing, but clearly, in this case, the local politician really did have significant "connections."

But while I've seen many people escaping trouble because of whom they know, what about the innocent people convicted and imprisoned? How many are there?

CHAPTER TWENTY-FIVE

INNOCENCE PROJECTIONS

Ever since I was a police officer and worked that sexual assault case in New Jersey where we were pretty much sold on the guilt of an innocent man, I've wondered how many innocent people were in prison.

The National Registry of Exonerations, a project of the University of Michigan Law School, maintains an ongoing count of those exonerated since 1989. When I say exonerated, I'm referring to individuals who were convicted of a crime they did not commit and were imprisoned. In other words, these are not "technically innocent" people freed because of some mistake in the trial or investigation. These are actual innocent people, people convicted of a crime they did not commit. The exoneration freed them from their prison cell. As of the beginning of February 2016, one thousand, seven hundred, and thirty-three (1,733) exonerations were listed. (http://www.law.umich.edu/special/exoneration)

(I say "the exoneration freed them from their prison cell." That's usually true. One exoneration in Florida doesn't fit that description. Frank Lee Smith was convicted of Murder and Rape in 1986. He spent 14 years on Death Row, before dying of cancer. Six months after his death, DNA testing proved Frank Lee Smith was innocent and identified the actual Murderer and Rapist.)

The list of exonerations is not all-inclusive and relies on voluntary reporting by attorneys and other interested parties. Therefore, it's a reasonable assumption that the actual number of exonerations is higher.

Of the 1,733 exonerated, 689 are Caucasian, 807 are Black, and 200 are Hispanic.

Per the registry's review of exonerations, 424 innocent people were sentenced to life or life without parole. Other sentences include 90, 95, and 99 years. One innocent person was sentenced to 100 years. One was sentenced to 148 years. One was sentenced to 172 years. **And 117 were sentenced to death.** Makes you wonder how many innocent people have been executed, doesn't it? There's probably no way we will ever know, but I'm sure it's happened more times than most of us care to think about.

So, does anyone know a good approximation of how many innocent people have been sent to jail? I have spoken to criminal justice experts from all over the country, and no one can say for sure. Some believe it could be as much as two and a half percent of convicts are innocent. Some say it's likely less than a half of one percent. An official at the Bureau of Justice Statistics for the U.S. Department of Justice told me that they have not conducted research to attempt to determine how many innocent people might be in jail and have no plans to do so. They directed me to the National Institute of Justice (NIJ) where I found that research had been conducted on what causes the wrongful conviction of innocent people, but the NIJ has no estimate of the percentage or number of innocent people likely in jail or prison.

According to the latest statistics offered by the Bureau of Justice Statistics, at the end of 2013, there was an estimated 6,899,000 offenders supervised by the adult correctional system in the United States. That includes offenders in prison, on parole, or on probation.

The International Centre for Prison Studies, a research center at the University of Essex in the United Kingdom, reports that the United States is the world leader in incarceration per capita. "Incarceration per capita" refers only to the number of people actually in prison.

As of 2013, the US held 716 prisoners per 100,000 people. For comparison, Russia imprisons 490 per 100,000 people, Australia 133, China 124, France 103, United Kingdom 103, Germany 78, Netherlands 75, and India 30. See the latest list for yourself at www.**prisonstudies**.org.

None of our allies, or our adversaries, comes even close to the U.S. when it comes to putting people in prison. Any way you look at it, we're doing something wrong.

Regarding private prisons: as more and more "private" prisons come on line, it must be remembered that these prisons make money based on the number of inmates in custody: the head count. I'm told some of their contracts even guarantee minimum head counts. Clearly, the private prisons need prisoners to make money. Those private prisons employ lobbyists in each state capital and in Washington, DC. Millions and millions of dollars are spent in those lobbying efforts. What do you think they're lobbying for? You can bet they're lobbying for more prisoners to house. The number of prisoners incarcerated in private prisons in the US has increased more than 1,600 percent since 1990. Google "political donations made by private prison industry" and see for yourself. It is disturbing and not the way our justice system should function, but that should be the subject of another book.

Getting back to the issue of innocence, if two and a half percent of those in custody are innocent, the number of innocent people in some form of custody at the end of 2013, be it imprisonment, parole, or probation, would be in excess of 172,000. If the number of innocent is just one half of one percent of those in some form of custody, the total number of innocent people in the system at the end of 2013 is over 34,000.

I believe the number of innocent people in prison, jail, probation, or parole in the U.S. might be well over two and a half percent and could easily represent more than 200,000 innocent people in some form of custody.

"Post-Conviction DNA Testing and Wrongful Conviction," is a 2012 study funded by the National Institute of Justice, Office of Justice Programs, U.S. Department of Justice (DOJ Contract Number 2008F-08165), conducted by John Roman, Ph.D., Kelly Walsh,Ph.D., Pamela Lachman, and Jennifer Yahner. All are associated with the Urban Institute's Justice Policy Center in Washington, DC. (www.urban.org)

In their study, which included a review of over half a million cases in the state of Virginia, 422 sexual assault convictions were identified between 1973 and 1987 in which evidence containing DNA was retained by the Virginia Division of Forensic Science. (Some of those sexual assaults also included murder.) Following DOJ-accepted procedures, the evidence was tested, and some startling data emerged.

In 40 out of those 422 convictions, the convicted offender was eliminated as the source of the questioned evidence. That's in excess of nine percent.

In 33 out of those same 422 convictions, the convicted offender was not only eliminated as the source of the questioned evidence, but that elimination could be shown to support exoneration. That's almost eight percent of that 422.

While this study does not claim to project the percentage of innocent people in jail throughout the nation, it certainly suggests that many, many thousands of innocent people are in prison.

In the April 2014 landmark study "Rate of False Conviction of Criminal Defendants Who Are Sentenced to Death," published in the Proceedings of the National Academy of Sciences by Samuel R. Gross, Professor at the University of Michigan Law School; Barbara O'Brien, an Associate Professor at Michigan State University College of Law; Chen Hu, of the American College of Radiology Clinical Research Center; and Edward H. Kennedy, of the Department of Biostatistics and Epidemiology, University of Pennsylvania School of Medicine, the authors conclude, "The rate of erroneous conviction of innocent criminal defendants is often described as not merely unknown but unknowable. We use survival analysis to model this effect, and estimate that if all death-sentenced defendants remained under sentence of death indefinitely at least 4.1% would be exonerated. We conclude that this is a conservative estimate of the proportion of false convictions among death sentences in the United States." (www.pnas.org)

Law enforcement agencies are overworked and underfunded. They can't afford to devote the personnel and expertise used in a capital murder investigation to every felony they investigate. They don't have the resources. Corners are sometimes cut. Shortcuts are sometimes taken. Mistakes occur. Therefore, since it's argued that 4.1% of those tried for capital crimes are innocent, wouldn't a similar percentage of those convicted of non-capital cases be innocent? Or would it be a higher percentage?

Crimes having the potential of a death sentence receive more scrutiny than other crimes, much more scrutiny. Those capital crime cases, the ones studied by Professor Gross, Professor O'Brien, and their colleagues, are held to a higher standard of investigative and judicial review. Further, statistically, a person known to the victim commits most murders, thus making smaller the suspect pool. That is not necessarily the case in other violent crimes. So, in most murders, with the field of potential perpetrators usually smaller and more manageable, and with the added scrutiny accompanying capital crime cases, there's less room for error. Additionally, detectives go to great lengths to clear homicides, leaving no stone unturned. It seems those death penalty cases should produce fewer errors resulting in wrongful convictions.

With that thought in mind, isn't it logical that "lesser," non-capital cases, the cases that do not always receive the same attention to detail, the same expenditure of the law enforcement agency's resources, the benefit of the law enforcement agency's best investigators, and the in-depth scrutiny of the prosecutor, would produce more errors and result in more wrongful convictions? It certainly makes sense to me. However, it is certainly possible that death penalty cases are more likely to result in false convictions than other crimes, as there is so much pressure on the investigators and prosecutors to win those cases.

Either way, if over four percent of inmates sentenced to death are innocent, it is logical to believe non-death penalty cases would at least approach that same rate of error, resulting in the conviction of innocent people at a rate approaching four percent. If that's true, well over 200,000 innocent people in the United States are in prison or some form of custody.

And finally, my old friend Dr. Patrick McManimon, Criminal Justice Program Coordinator at Kean University, New Jersey, provided me with his perspective: "Wrongful conviction has more to do with plea bargaining than exhaustive investigation. Ninety percent of all criminal cases are resolved by plea-bargaining, and the trial tax is really the tool that entices confessions. cases rarely see the light of day, and as a result, the justice meted out is compromised." (Those plea bargains by innocent people are not counted when figuring wrongful conviction estimates, they are in addition to those convictions and, if factored in, would add many thousand to the wrongfully convicted estimates.)

The fact that the vast majority of Cases are plea-bargained does not lessen the number of innocent people going to prison. When faced with false eyewitness identification, many a defendant will succumb to the prosecutor's (and defense attorney's) offer for a far lesser sentence than rolling the dice, going to trial, losing, and spending many more years behind bars. It's a lose-lose scenario. Unfortunately, it happens all the time.

The existing research pointing to innocent people going to jail certainly justifies an examination of how wrongful convictions occur and mandates appropriate changes to correct the system producing those wrongful convictions.

CHAPTER TWENTY-SIX

CAUSES OF WRONGFUL CONVICTIONS

The Innocence Project (http://www.innocenceproject.org) identifies the causes of wrongful convictions as:

- Eyewitness Misidentification
- Not Validated or Improper Forensic Science
- False Confessions/Admissions
- Government Misconduct
- (Bad) Informants
- Bad Lawyering

My experiences in the last 30 years validates those findings. The following explains each of the listed causes.

EYEWITNESS MISIDENTIFICATION

In 553 of the 1,733 exonerations recorded by the National Registry of Exonerations, mistaken witness identification was a factor. And in nearly 75% of the wrongful convictions overturned by DNA evidence, mistaken witness identification played a pivotal role. It is the single most prevalent factor leading to false convictions.

Great import is placed on the testimony of eyewitnesses. In many courtroom trials, eyewitness testimony is the only "substantive" or non-circumstantial testimony offered and is the primary reason for conviction. That is problematic in that the certainty by which an eyewitness identifies a suspect has no relationship to the identification's accuracy, nor does the detail a witness conveys. Just because someone is sure they're identifying the right person doesn't mean that they are any more accurate than the witness who says, "I think that's him." Additionally, cross-race identification is particularly difficult. For example, if you're black, you generally don't remember and recognize white people as well as you remember and recognize fellow black people. The overriding memory is the fact that the person was a different color than you. It's true for all races and makes visual identification of suspects challenging.

Many people believe memory acts like a camera or video recorder. That's not the case.

Memories of faces are reconstructed from clues that reside in several places in the brain. Sometimes, those clues, intentionally or not, come from the police or prosecutor. Without intending to, an investigator or prosecutor may provide clues to the suspected perpetrator's appearance that become logged into the witness's mind and become a memory of what the witness thought he or she observed.

Eyewitness identification is usually obtained through a lineup, which can be conducted by an actual "lineup" of six people (as you often see in many movies and TV shows, but in reality is hardly ever used), or more frequently through the viewing of a photo lineup, which traditionally is a compilation of six photographs on a single sheet where the photo of the suspect is randomly placed amongst five other photos of individuals bearing similar characteristics.

All lineups need to be consistent and fair. The suspect should not be in any way highlighted. In some cases, the suspect appears on glossy photo paper, while the five "fillers" are featured with matte finish photo paper. Sometimes, the "fillers" are standard police booking photos, while the suspect's photo is taken in a more casual, non-structured setting. Those situations highlight the suspect, lead to false identifications, and should invalidate any identification.

Another issue revolves around the presentation of the photo lineup. When the investigator hands the folder containing six photographs, sometimes known as a "six-pack," to the witness, non-verbal communication may be occurring without the knowledge of the investigator or the witness. The investigator's visual focus may inadvertently "point out" the suspect. The way the six-pack is handled may somehow highlight the suspect. The whole process is rife with potential flaws.

Randy Means is an attorney who for 25 years has been a partner in a nationally recognized law enforcement training and consulting company. For 20 years Randy was also the primary legal and risk management trainer for the International Association of Chiefs of Police (IACP) and has provided training at multiple national conferences of the FBI National Academy Associates. Randy is also the past head of the National Association of Police Legal Advisors and has provided instruction in every state in the U.S. and Canada. I have tremendous respect for Randy, his opinions, and his awareness of cutting-edge law enforcement issues.

I asked Randy to review all the recommendations I make in this chapter. After reviewing my recommendations, Randy advised me he agreed with them all except my witness identification recommendations. After reviewing Randy's take on the issue, I deleted my explanations of the best eye-witness procedures and have provided Randy's. They make more sense.

Randy stated, "I think you should recommend that we not use body lineups at all (we haven't anyway for about 30 years, as you noted) nor should we ever use a single six pack – for the same reason in both cases. In either case, the eyewitness (who knows our suspect must be in the array, despite our statement that he may not be, or why are we doing this at all) will be trying to find the guy in the lineup who looks the most like the perpetrator. Obviously, even if the eyewitness "succeeds" in this endeavor, this is not a good identification process."

Randy continued, adding his logical solution to this identification problem: "I think you should recommend that all lineups be photo lineups and that all of them should be conducted by sequential one-at-a-time presentation of a large number (like 20-30) photos without the eyewitness knowing how many photos there will be. In fact, we should tell the eyewitness that there will be a large number of photos, that the suspect may or may not be among them, and that they eyewitness will not know when the end of the presentation is coming – at a point we'll simply say, "that's it." If no one has been identified, then so be it – and that's the end of the line. If the eyewitness wants to try again, we would use all the same photos as in the first sequential display, with additional (new) photos interspersed (increasing the overall number of photos by quite a few) and with a shuffling of the deck."

Randy added, "Any use of a six pack display would be a sequential display of multiple six packs (maybe 4-5) with instructions to the eyewitness that we will be showing him or her a large number of pictures, presented six at a time, that a suspect may or may not be among them, and that the eyewitness will not know when the process is coming to an end until we say, "that's all."

The only reason I'm suggesting the use of six packs at all is because a lot of photo array software is set up for six packs – our traditional arrangement.

So, under this recommendation, we would never use a single six pack approach."

The fairness and quest for accuracy offered by Randy's suggestions make great sense and would provide very strong evidence when an identification is made. As with other identification procedures, the entire process should be video recorded.

My home state of New Jersey is ahead of its time with regard to eyewitness testimony. In 2011, the New Jersey Supreme Court declared New Jersey's standards for eyewitness testimony were unreliable. (State v. Henderson; 2011 N.J. Lexis 927, 8/24/11)

In their decision, the N.J. Supreme Court examined scientific research on eyewitness identification and found current practices were not reliable and did not deter inappropriate law enforcement conduct. They also determined that the entire process gave the jury the impression that they should be able to judge the reliability of the eyewitnesses' testimony even though they do not have the innate capability of doing so. The court ruled that the scientifically based pros and cons of eyewitness identification be thoroughly explained to the jury when eyewitness testimony is employed. That explanation must offer these questions the jury should consider:

- Was the lineup administered using a third-party (double blind) process and was the witness advised that the actual suspect may or may not be in the lineup?

- Did the police not provide feedback suggesting the witness selected was the "right" person?

- Did the police make notes on the witness's level of confidence in making the identification?

- Was the witness exposed to the suspect on multiple occasions, which would highlight the person as the likely correct suspect in the lineup?

- Was the witness under a high level of stress when witnessing the crime?

- Was a weapon used?

- How much time did the witness have to observe the suspect?

- How far was the witness from the suspect when viewed, and what were the light conditions?

- Was the witness exposed to factors that would make the identification more difficult, such as the mental state of the witness, was the witness using alcohol or drugs, or were there eyesight impediments, etc.?

- Did the suspect appear to be wearing a disguise at the time of the crime, or did the suspect have different facial features at the time of the crime, such a beard, mustache, dyed hair, etc.?

- What was the length of time between the crime and the identification?

- Was the witness of a different race that the suspect?

These questions, and the explanations associated with them, encourage law enforcement to follow progressive guidelines, including the video recording of the entire identification procedure, to insure that the identification process is conducted in the most accurate and just way possible. New Jersey's identification standards should be embraced throughout the U.S. as being in justice's best interest.

A note on video recording: Video recording the interviews of suspects, as well as witnesses, allows the jury to observe the demeanor and behavior of the investigator(s) conducting the interviews. In the case of witnesses, the jury can observe for themselves how the information obtained was accomplished without inappropriately leading or suggestive questions, observations, or coercion. In the case of suspects, video recording of the entire interview, from start to finish, demonstrates the voluntary nature of the interaction between suspect and interviewer, as well as the specific, detailed information obtained. The video recording ultimately becomes the prosecution's best evidence as to the strength of the evidence and the likely culpability of the suspect.

I believe the time will come when the majority, if not all, of police interactions with the public are recorded, capturing critical incidents, arrests and most every other facet of the police officer's profession. And, as select videos are made available to the public, the public will finally see how very difficult it can be to be a police officer and how most officers are there to serve the public and do so with bravery and integrity. It will also allow for the demonstration of the unfiltered police officer's perspective of incidents, rather the potentially incomplete and out of context video provided by nearby witnesses or accomplices. The police-worn cameras clearly demonstrate transparency and accuracy by the police employing those cameras.

Video recorders attached to officer's collars or on special glasses were tested in Rialto, California, in 2012. A year after the implementation, use of force by officers fell by almost 60 percent. Further, complaints against officers fell an amazing 88 percent. (Zack Peterson, Tampa Bay Times, 7/5/14) Sounds like a no-brainer that the police and the public would be well served by police wearing video recorders.

The presence of the camera can have a cooling effect on everyone present. Officers are less likely to encounter physically hostile resistance when the potentially violent individual knows a camera is watching. It can also cool the officer in those heated moments that sometimes unnecessarily escalate to violence.

A suspect I was taking into custody once punched and fought with me. While I attempted to place him in handcuffs, he continued to fight, and I was forced to take him to the ground, causing his head to hit the sidewalk and bleed. I did what was appropriate in the situation, using only necessary force and immediately rendered appropriate first-aid, but was still concerned that the guy might have sustained a head injury that would result in him requiring hospitalization and then, with the help of a handy personal injury or civil rights attorney, the filing of a complaint against me. I would have paid for a video recording of the incident, as that would have quickly demonstrated the subject's assault on me followed by my proper reaction and justified use of force.

I've read that police departments in the U.S. pay approximately $2 Billion in department liability costs and settlements annually. The embracing of this new video technology throughout the country will save the departments and officers' money and prevent many unnecessary complaints. In the long run, it's good for the public and good for the police.

NOT VALIDATED OR IMPROPER FORENSIC SCIENCE

In 49 percent of DNA-related exonerations and roughly 25 percent of all exonerations, not validated or improper forensic science contributed to wrongful convictions. (In most cases, DNA testing is not an option because no evidence containing DNA is recovered from the crime scene.)

While DNA is absolutely accurate, in many states, some so-called scientific techniques are employed but not scientifically validated, such as hair and fiber comparisons. Great import is given to hair comparison, which ultimately is not nearly as definitive as once thought, though it's still sometimes good for determining racial group, the identification of added chemicals, i.e. dye or bleach, and sometimes as a source of

DNA, if the hair root is available. In 2012, the Justice Department announced it was conducting a review of thousands of criminal cases, dating back to 1985, where hair and fiber analysis led to convictions. Inquiries determined a lack of consistency in the examination of hair and fibers and pointed out that any two hair and fiber experts might not agree on the other's findings.

Adding to the problem are identification experts who sometimes testify to "facts" that are without clear scientific basis. In rare circumstances, forensic specialists have actually engaged in misconduct, providing prosecution-supporting testimony without basis. That behavior is rare, but must be considered.

Ultimately, the solution is appropriate scientific oversight and government-funded research to validate standard forensic methods, tests, and testimony.

FALSE CONFESSION/ADMISSION

People occasionally confess to crimes they did not commit. As counterintuitive as that might sound, it's a fact. The reasons are varied. Sometimes, the person is mentally unstable due to mental illness or substance abuse, and in trying to please, they'll say anything they're asked to say. Sometimes, an intensive interrogation/interview leads the person into agreeing to anything the interviewer says, just to get the interview over. Sometimes, the interviewee thinks it's in his best interest, based on what the person conducting the interview says or "sells" to him. Sometimes, the interviewee is drunk or high during the interview and willing to confess to anything. Sometimes, details of the crime are inadvertently supplied to the interviewee by the interviewing officer and end up being seen later as an admission when the interviewee repeats what he's been told. Sometimes, the interviewee is scared of the interviewer and feels threatened into providing a false confession.

In 221 of the 1,733 reported exonerations, false confessions contributed to the conviction.

There's a simple solution to the issue. Record all custodial interviews. The whole interview. From the interview's start until its conclusion, the conversation should be recorded and, preferably, captured on video. Let the judge and jury hear and see what was said.

There was a time when people would argue that the cost and inconvenience of recording all such interviews would be prohibitive. Not anymore. High quality recording capability resides in most smart phones, and digital recorders are inexpensive. Ultimately, a recording provides the best evidence to play for a jury and prevents allegations of police harassment or mistreatment, as the recording gives proof of how a suspect was treated while being interviewed. It also proves to the jury what the subject actually said, preventing the defense attorney from claiming his client's words were misquoted or misconstrued. It's in the best interest of justice for both the prosecution and the defense.

In some states, recording of custodial interviews/interrogations is mandatory. In 2014, the US Department of Justice made the recording of custodial interviews required by DOJ enforcement agencies, including the FBI, DEA, BATF and the Marshal's Service. Once the practice is in place, many investigators recognize it as a valuable tool and embrace its use. It really should be the standard for all law enforcement agencies. It's the best evidence of what was actually said.

In my interview of Marcus Hamilton back in 1987, I did not have the benefit of recording the interview. At the time, the FBI simply didn't record interviews. I wish we had, as Special Agent Phil Stukes and I spent a long time developing rapport to get Marcus to tell us about killing the victim, and the jury would have heard a pleasant, even friendly conversation that resulted in Marcus Hamilton admitting to a horrific killing. The defense tried to suppress the confession in a pre-trial hearing, but the confession was ruled as voluntary and was presented to the jury. There would be no need for a suppression hearing if the interview was recorded. If for some reason the confession had been suppressed, there's no telling if Marcus would have been convicted. Recording interviews really makes good sense and is in the best interest of justice.

GOVERNMENT MISCONDUCT

I've been around law enforcement all of my life. My older brother David retired a captain after 28 years on the Princeton Township (NJ) Police Department. He was my role model and inspired me to pursue a law enforcement career. Also, my grandfather was a long-time Princeton Borough police detective, who even did some counter-espionage preliminary inquiries for the FBI during World War II. (I've got the letters.) I'm a Life Member of the International Association of Chiefs of Police (IACP). Between my police, NCIS, and FBI experience, I know and have worked with law enforcement officers all over the country. The overwhelming majority of police officers are professionals who work in an ethical and honest manner seeking justice while endeavoring to take violent people and people who prey on the public off the street.

However, misconduct sometimes occurs. Investigators conveying improper suggestions to witnesses while conducting eyewitness identifications occasionally happen. False confessions are sometimes solicited through coercion, especially from the vulnerable and mentally challenged. Unreliable and/or untested informants are sometimes employed and given credibility that has not been earned. Rarely, officers take the stand and intentionally mislead jurors.

And, occasionally, prosecutors don't provide the defense with information that might actually clear or cast doubt on the guilt of the defendant. That's called a Brady Violation.

In the 1963 Supreme Court case of Brady v. Maryland (373 U.S. 83), the court held that the withholding of exculpatory evidence violates due process. Basically, if the prosecution has evidence that tends to show the innocence of the defendant or information that might mitigate the punishment for the defendant, such information must be provided to the defense. "Brady Violations" occur when the defense is not provided exculpatory information. In my experience, it happens far too often. I recently exchanged emails with Professor Samuel Gross, one of the founders of the National Registry of Exonerations, about quantifying Brady Violations in the National Registry's database, and Professor Gross advised they have recently started a project to do just that. It's important to see the scope of Brady Violations, but it's more important to do something about it.

As it stands now, Brady Violations are routinely ignored, as the prosecutor normally enjoys some form of immunity. In reality, intentionally withholding exculpatory evidence should result in dire consequences. Again, it's a matter of fundamental fairness to the sometimes-innocent defendant. Seems logical to me, but of course, I'm not an attorney.

Ultimately, there needs to be appropriate reforms to check government misconduct. Some of the solutions/suggestions I've mentioned in this book, such as recording interviews, would be a good start.

INFORMANTS

In 963 of the 1,733 exonerations recorded by the National Registry of Exonerations, perjury or false accusations were a factor. That represents more than 55 percent of the total exonerations reported. The number of those who were informants providing false information is not specified, but you can be sure that unscrupulous "jailhouse informants" have put a lot of innocent people in jail. Those jailhouse informants are criminals, after all, and they often have much to gain by lying about what they heard or were told, and feel they owe no allegiance to the person on whom they're falsely informing.

As an NCIS agent and FBI agent, informants were essential to my success. I focused on finding them from the start of my law enforcement career, and they treated me well. My favorites were ones who would provide me information as to the whereabouts of people I was hunting and those who got close to individuals committing crimes and were able to provide verbatim testimony or recordings of the suspect. They were, for the most part, quid pro quo informants, who were paid cash on verifiable delivery of useful information. There was little room for the informant to provide false information and still get paid.

As a new agent in the FBI, I quickly learned that the FBI had rules and regulations you had to follow in order to operate informants, and that FBI supervisors were responsible for verifying that informants functioned correctly. Strict records were maintained, and the supervisors were mandated to ensure the government was getting its "bang for the buck," as informants were paid. Supervisors also had to occasionally meet informants face to face to ensure the informant was being handled appropriately. Detailed documentation of information provided by the informant was thoroughly reviewed, and each informant was evaluated on a regular basis to make a determination if the informant was still appropriate for use. I'm aware of instances of informants gone wild in the FBI, but those are aberrations and not reflective of the in-depth oversight normally provided informants by FBI management.

Jailhouse informants require particularly strict oversight. Their motivation must be acknowledged and their information independently verified to be useful. After all, the fact that they are in jail does not lend much to their credibility. As I mentioned earlier, while in Houston, I obtained an unlawful flight warrant for a suspect who had shot and nearly killed two Houston police officers. After the fugitive was taken into custody, his cellmate was able to record him bragging that he was "not going to do any serious time" because his father was very wealthy. The cellmate/informant was able to record that information, and it was played for the judge and jury. If I recall correctly, that wealthy young man was sentenced to 99 years in prison.

So, a jailhouse informant capable of recording conversations is a potent informant. Problem is, how do you record conversations while in jail? With today's technology and miniaturization of recording devices, it's not that hard to do. And it is certainly the best evidence.

Otherwise, how credible is a guy who's in jail when he testifies? Since jailhouse informants are known to frequently lie under oath, several factors must be weighed. Has the informant been paid to testify? Is the testimony being offered to lessen his sentence or get him out of jail altogether? Has he testified multiple times, and does he always seem to be in the right place to capture a defendant offering incriminating statements? Basically, jailhouse informants shouldn't be trusted without independent corroboration, such as a recording of the subject's incriminating statements.

Informants on the street must also be frequently evaluated; their reliability must be documented and the informants subjected to regular supervisory oversight. Every law enforcement agency should adhere to standard practices for the operation of informants to insure their information is properly evaluated and their veracity substantiated. Those standards should be fashioned after models established by respected law enforcement organizations, such as CALEA (The Commission on Accreditation for Law Enforcement Agencies) and the IACP (International Association of Chiefs of Police.)

BAD LAWYERING

In 403 of the 1,733 exonerations reported by the National Registry of Exonerations, inadequate legal defense was a factor in the defendant being found guilty. The Innocence Project reports on a review of convictions overturned by DNA testing and found some pretty disturbing behaviors by defense attorneys who have:

- Slept in the courtroom during trial
- Been disbarred shortly after finishing a death penalty case
- Failed to investigate alibis
- Failed to call or consult experts on forensic issues
- Failed to show up for hearings

Anecdotally, I've heard some pretty outrageous stories. One innocent individual I know was convicted of murder and spent over 25 years in prison before being exonerated through DNA testing. During trial, he was represented by an attorney who knew his client's girlfriend was sleeping with one of the homicide investigators on the case, but didn't see fit to bring that up in trial.

While the state must prove "beyond a reasonable doubt" that the defendant is guilty, the state has great advantages. For starters, many jurors believe from the start of a trial that the defendant must be guilty or the state wouldn't have charged him. Additionally, in cases handled by public defenders, the state has far more investigative and legal resources than the defense.

Sometimes, the defense attorney is simply overwhelmed and without the experience or resources to provide a proper defense as guaranteed by the 6th Amendment. The 6th Amendment includes the statement, "the accused shall…have the assistance of counsel for his defense." I bet George Mason and John Locke, the authors of the 6th Amendment, were assuming "counsel" would be "competent" when penning that amendment. Likely, from their perspective, they could assume that any attorney passing the bar would be competent. Of course, in the 18th century, the United States was not home to over a million attorneys. It was a much simpler time.

Problem:
Tight state budgets for public defenders sometimes result in inadequate defense.

The result:
Frequently, clients plead to crimes not committed to avoid "rolling the dice" in court, resulting in substantially longer sentences. Occasionally innocent people are convicted and sent to prison because of inadequate legal representation. Occasionally innocent people are sent to death row.

The fix:
Nationwide legislative reform to make our criminal justice system operate on a more level playing field, with adequate funding for defense attorneys to provide constitutionally-mandated assistance of counsel for the defendant's defense. (In those cases, felony and misdemeanor, which could result in prison time.)

With government finances so tight, that's not an easy fix. One way to address that is to focus our criminal justice system on crimes that matter and get out of spending so much money and time on drug investigations. Prisons shouldn't be filled with drug offenders integrated with violent offenders. The long-term result is incredibly taxing on our resources and can't help but produce an influx of new violent offenders. Possession of user quantities of illegal drugs should result in a civil citation or ticket to clear those thousands and thousands of cases out of our criminal courts. Reform is needed. Additionally, plea-bargaining should be closely examined. In an effort to provide the best service to the maximum number of clients, overworked public defenders sometimes consider a good plea bargain a win for their client and sell it as such. Problem is, it's not a win if the client is innocent.

For a detailed look at reasons why the innocent are convicted, I recommend, "False Justice: Eight Myths that Convict the Innocent," by Jim and Nancy Petro.

CHAPTER TWENTY-SEVEN

THE BOTTOM LINE

The vast majority of people convicted and sent to prison are guilty, but thousands aren't.

Can we stand idly by and allow thousands of innocent people to languish in prison for crimes they did not commit?

Should we tolerate a certain percentage of innocent people being executed?

The answer to both questions is a resounding NO. Innocent people must not be written off as an unavoidable by-product of our criminal justice system. We're better than that. We can and must make our criminal justice system a more level playing field.

We must set standards for eyewitness identification and require law enforcement to stick to them.

We must recognize that invalidated and improper forensic science exists and set appropriate nationwide scientific oversight to address and correct those issues.

We must record all subject interviews, in their entirety, so the judge and jury can understand the circumstances when confessions occur.

We must address, through appropriate oversight, the issues of government misconduct and take appropriate action to correct/discourage such behavior.

We must ensure the validity of informant's information with appropriate oversight, making certain it is in accordance with recognized acceptable standards.

We must address the issue of bad lawyering. Sufficient funds must be made available to provide competent defense for defendants unable to pay for legal representation in felony and serious misdemeanor cases. The prosecution should not enjoy economic and personnel advantages over the defense attorneys they face.

We must overhaul the plea bargaining process to avoid sending innocent people to prison.

We must examine the issue of whom we're sending to jail and stop incarcerating non-violent offenders.

The recommendations I endorse are not difficult to implement. They will have an economic impact, but that is necessary if we're to be a just nation. They are the right things to do, not only for the innocent, but also for the victims.

For every time an innocent person goes to jail for a crime of violence, it's likely a guilty, violent and dangerous person walks free.

THANKS

My experiences in the criminal justice arena have been greatly influenced by many people I've met along the way. The late Montgomery Township Police Chief Mike Szoke was an innovative, professional police officer who gave me my first law enforcement position. He was a good, forward thinking man who passed on to me many important lessons.

While with NIS, I worked with some great people, including Ed Scully, the Security Director at the Portsmouth Naval Shipyard, and William Mortimer, the Chief of Detectives and later the Police Commissioner for the Portsmouth, NH, Police Department. Ed and Mort were two of the nicest and most professional people with whom I've worked.

In the FBI, there have been too many people to count who have helped me along the way. However, I mention a few. Ken Neu was my first supervisor in the FBI. He was tough, smart, demanding and probably the best supervisor a new agent could have. Jack Hunt was my boss in Phoenix and during one of my FBIHQ assignments. He had a vision of intelligence-driven investigation that, while not quickly adapted, was exactly what the Bureau needed. Sheri Farrar and Mark Bullock were Assistant Directors I worked for and learned from. Both were excellent at their jobs, demanding, fair, and results oriented. And, I thank the late Merrill Parks, my ASAC in Houston and my friend thereafter. He always provided good advice, had a wonderful sense of humor, and was a great man.

And to Seth Miller and the staff of the Innocence Project of Florida who, for minimal renumeration, do tremendous work to aid the innocent.

And to James Bain and William Dillon, two innocent men, freed from life sentences, who have taught me much about foregiveness and dignity.

And thanks to my friend of over 50 years, Dr. Patrick McManimon, who conducted the first edit of this manuscript.

And thanks to Frankie and the late Joe Thomas for always being there for the Cromwell's.

And I thank my sister, Kim Cromwell, who has been my friend, counselor and confidant throughout most my life.

And to my three sons, Michael, Daniel and Johnny. I know it was tough making all those moves, but you guys sure turned out well and I'm very proud of each of you.

And to my three grandchildren, Spiro, Sofia and Joe. You make me smile, make me proud, and make me really appreciate being a grandparent.

I've been a witness to the American system of justice at the local, state, and federal level for over 30 years. Our country was founded on a vision of equal justice for all. We haven't attained that vision. It is something that should be of concern to all who believe that truth and justice go hand in hand. The simple recommendations I present in this book can help us along that road to a more level playing field for everyone who finds him/herself subjected to our criminal justice system.